# A Man After God's Own Heart

## A DEVOTIONAL

## JIM GEORGE

HARVEST HOUSE PUBLISHERS
EUGENE, OREGON

*Cover by Aesthetic Soup, Nashville, Tennessee*

**A MAN AFTER GOD'S OWN HEART—A DEVOTIONAL**
Copyright © 2012 Jim George
Published by Harvest House Publishers
Eugene, Oregon 97402
www.harvesthousepublishers.com

ISBN 978-0-7369-5972-8 (hardcover)
ISBN 978-0-7369-5973-5 (eBook)

**Printed in China**

15 16 17 18 19 20 21 22 / RDS-CD / 10 9 8 7 6 5 4 3 2 1

# A Note from Jim

In my earlier books *A Man After God's Own Heart* and *A Husband After God's Own Heart,* I pointed to Acts 13:22 to explain what it means to follow after God's heart. God states, "I have found David the son of Jesse, a man after My own heart, who will do all My will." Now, David wasn't perfect. In fact, he was far from perfect! But God saw something in his heart. God saw a man who had a heart that, when confronted by God, desired to correct his ways and get back on track with Him. Though David was less than ideal, he was still fully committed to progressing in his desire to follow God.

It is my prayer that this practical book of exhortations and inspirational thoughts will help you remember that God is not looking for perfection. All He asks for is a man who is progressing in his desire to become a man after God's own heart.

*Jim George*

# Taking Your
# Decisions to God

Every major accomplishment in a man's life requires a high level of commitment. I'm sure you can remember such an accomplishment in your life. Perhaps you were starting your own business. Or you were considering a job change or mapping out a new direction for your company or family. Whatever it was, you probably felt some initial hesitancy. One day you were eager to start…and the next you weren't so sure. But once you made the decision to proceed, all the long hours of effort were worth it because of the joy of seeing the fruit of your labors.

What major decision or change are you facing right now? Have you included God in the planning process? Take time to pray and share your thoughts and concerns with Him, and ask for His leading as you move forward.

*God, I commit my plans to You today. Help me to honor You in all I do. Thank You for guiding me so that my decisions will glorify You and bless the people around me. Amen.*

# The Price of Commitment

King David understood the necessity of pouring himself fully into his commitments. When it came time to obtain land so he could build an altar to God, someone offered to give David some land for free. But David knew that the greater the commitment, the greater would be the blessing. Therefore he declared he would not offer burnt offerings to God "with that which costs me nothing" (2 Samuel 24:24).

David declined what was convenient, and expressed his love and commitment to God through personal sacrifice. In what ways have you recently expressed your level of commitment to the Lord? Have there been costs involved? You will reap blessings as you wholeheartedly follow God and do what He says. Consider what God said about David: "I have found [him]...a man after My own heart, who will do all My will" (Acts 13:22).

*God, strengthen me so that when my commitment is put to the test, I won't falter. Help me to be a man of my word in my relationships with others and with You. Amen.*

# God Looks
# at the Heart

When God sent the prophet Samuel to look for a new king for Israel, He cautioned him, "The LORD does not see as man sees; for man looks at the outward appearance, but the LORD looks at the heart" (1 Samuel 16:7). In everything, God looks on the heart. Your relationship with Him has to do with your heart and your heart's desire. As happened with King David, you may experience lapses in your walk with God. We all do! But whenever that happened, David always returned to God in obedience. That's what made him a man after God's own heart.

Does that describe you as well? No matter what happens, is the deepest desire of your heart to yield yourself fully to Him in obedience? If yes, you'll become a man God can—and will—use.

*God, I'm amazed that You don't give up on me when I fail. I do want to walk in obedience, to be free from sin, and to see You move in and through my life. Amen.*

# What God Desires in You

David was a man with feet of clay, a man who committed sins that grieved God's heart. Yet over the long haul, he sought to be righteous, and his desire was to do God's will. This is the kind of man God looks for. David wasn't perfect, and he didn't deserve God's blessings. But in his heart he had the right desire—a longing to follow and please God.

Is that your personal longing as well? You may feel that being a man after God's heart is too lofty a goal because of some of your past actions. But remember: God looked at David's *heart*. And that's where He's going to look in your life as well. When it comes to becoming a man after God's heart, you can count on God's grace—a grace that enables and strengthens you at all times.

> *God, You know my heart better than I do. Help me to open my heart to You every day. Purify my heart, I pray, and renew me from the inside out. Amen.*

# Seek First
# His Kingdom

We hear a lot of talk about establishing priorities in our lives. But no one said it better than Jesus: "Do not worry, saying, 'What shall we eat?' or 'What shall we drink?' or 'What shall we wear?'...But seek first the kingdom of God and His righteousness, and all these things shall be added to you" (Matthew 6:31,33). Food, drink, and clothing are important, but they're not your first priority. Rather, your pursuit of God—and the resulting spiritual growth—is what really matters. When you put God first, He will provide for you and your family. That's His promise—seek Him, and He will take care of everything else. As C.S. Lewis said, "Put first things first and we get second things thrown in: put second things first and we lose both first and second things."

*Jesus, thank You for inviting me to seek Your kingdom. You are more than just my first priority—all my priorities find their rightful place in You and Your kingdom. Amen.*

# Yielding to God

When God looks at your life, what does He look for? Not perfection—being a Christian doesn't mean you don't sin anymore. Rather, it means sin is no longer the predominant pattern of your life. As a Christian, you are a new creature in Christ (2 Corinthians 5:17). And when you do sin, because the Holy Spirit lives in you, you are convicted and possess a desire to repent so the joy of your fellowship with God can be restored (Psalm 51:12).

God never asks you to do something without providing you with the enablement to do it. With the Holy Spirit's help, you can live as a man after God's own heart. As you yield your life fully to the Lord, the Spirit will produce fruit that is consistent with being a child of God.

*Lord, You can do anything—even make me a man after Your own heart. Thank You for forgiving me and for continuing to make me the man You want me to be. Amen.*

# Planted in God's Word

Just as water is the only thing that can relieve thirst in the desert, God's Word is the only thing that can satisfy our spiritual thirst. It alone can nourish us spiritually and help us grow as Christians.

So if you want to live as a man after God's own heart, you need to make sure you're firmly planted in God's Word. God has much to say about life and your priorities, and if you neglect the Bible, you will find yourself spiritually malnourished and drifting without direction in life.

If you want to live as a man after God's own heart, then there's no better place for you to go for guidance. Don't you agree? What impact is the Bible having on your life right now? What would making the Bible your first priority involve?

*Father, thank You for the Bible! Help me to never take for granted the opportunity to let Your Word shape my thinking, my speaking, and my actions. Amen.*

# The Keys to
# Your Growth

When it comes to spiritual growth, God doesn't leave you on your own. His Spirit, who lives in every believer, gives you the power and desire to grow. He is your Guide and Helper (John 14:16-17,26).

Between the Bible and the Holy Spirit, you have everything you need to grow spiritually. And the more you grow, the more God can use you. He can work through you to touch the lives of others—your wife, your children, your co-workers, your fellow churchgoers, your friends and neighbors.

Ultimately, if you want your life to count, you need to grow spiritually. And because Scripture offers everything you need for nourishment, it needs to remain top priority in your life. The more you crave God's Word, the more you'll grow and have an impact.

*Lord, thank You for giving me everything I need to continue growing more and more like You. Help me to never give up, never settle for less, and always rely on Your Word. Amen.*

# Making a
# Difference in Others

What's remarkable about spiritual growth is the way it can impact every area of your life. As you grow, you please God and become mature as a Christian, and you also see a positive effect on your relationships with others. Each of us, as Christian men, husbands, fathers, and workers, have contact with many people—people whose lives we can impact if we're growing spiritually.

If you want to be a strong, maturing man of God, your first priority is to develop a closer relationship with God. That means spending time with Him in prayer and in His Word. As you seek His guidance and wisdom, You'll give Him the opportunity to work through you so as to point others to Him. There's no better way to make your life count for all eternity.

*God, I'm amazed that You could use me to make a difference in other people's lives! Renew my heart and mind, I pray, and let Your life in me spill out onto everyone I meet. Amen.*

# Hungering After God's Word

John Wesley was greatly devoted to reading the Bible. He laid hold of the Bible because his heart's desire was to grow…and the Bible laid hold of him as well. Every year, he lifted up this prayer as a covenant to God, expressing his desire to grow:

> O blessed Jesus…You have been pleased to give me your holy laws as the Rule of my life…subscribing to all your laws as holy, just, and good, I solemnly take them as the Rule of my words, thoughts, and actions; promising that…I will endeavor to order and govern my whole life according to your direction…

When you commit yourself to growing spiritually and following God's Word, then God, by His grace, will enable you to fulfill all the responsibilities He has given you. Through His power, you'll accomplish great things for Him.

> *Lord, I confess that I can't fulfill Your vision for my life in my own strength. May Your Word and Your Spirit guide me today and empower me to do everything You've called me to do. Amen.*

# Staying
# Faithful

Spiritual growth is a lifelong pursuit. You grow in spiritual maturity moment by moment, day by day, year by year. It doesn't happen instantly—it is a steady but sure process that takes place over time and requires ongoing attention.

In many ways, spiritual exercise is a lot like physical exercise. When you stop exercising physically, your body might not show the results of inactivity for a while. But one day you'll wake up and find everything is sagging in the wrong places.

The same goes for your spiritual life. As you gradually neglect prayer and time in God's Word, at first you might not notice the effects. But they'll catch up to you eventually, and you'll find your spiritual productivity sagging. That's why it's so vital to remain steadfast even in the little things of the Christian life.

> Lord, being faithful in prayer and Bible reading
> day after day is sometimes difficult for me. Open
> my eyes so I can see the changes You want to make
> in my life and the progress we're making. Amen.

# First Things First

Every single day, you'll find yourself repeatedly having to make the choice between priorities and personal pursuits. Ultimately your decision will come down to this: Have I put God and His Word first? Have I taken care of my God-given responsibilities, or neglected them?

You'll find it helpful to invite the Lord to help you with your choices. Make a conscious effort to involve Him in your daily decisions. Take time to pray and communicate your thoughts. Ask Him if there are any biblical principles that might help you make a right decision. As you do all these things, you'll put Proverbs 3:5-6 to work in your life: "Trust in the Lord with all your heart, and lean not on your own understanding; in all your ways acknowledge Him, and He shall direct your paths."

*God, teach me how to acknowledge You in everything I do. Whenever I make a decision—big or little, consciously or subconsciously—help me to know the joy of putting You first. Amen.*

# Freedom from Sin's Effects

Jesus put the seriousness of sin into perspective when He said that even if you merely get angry with someone, you have committed murder in your heart (Matthew 5:22). And even if you lust after a woman in your mind, you have committed adultery with her in your heart (Matthew 5:28).

The bottom line is that any sin, whether big or small, overt or covert, is an affront to God and must be confessed and forsaken. Anytime you have unconfessed sin in your life, it will hurt your relationship with God, stunt your spiritual growth, and affect your loved ones and your work.

When you acknowledge your sin to God, you'll experience the wonderful cleansing that comes with confession: "*Blessed* is he whose transgression is forgiven, whose sin is covered" (Psalm 32:1).

> *Lord, I want to be more like You—free from sin.*
> *Show me ways that I've given sin a foothold in*
> *my life. Thank You for forgiving and cleansing*
> *me! Amen.*

# The Blessings of Growth

When it comes to spiritual growth, you can't rest on yesterday's progress. It's like eating food—your need for nourishment is constant, which means getting into your Bible daily and praying regularly.

If you're thinking, *That isn't easy!* you are right. While it's true growing spiritually mature requires action on your part, the benefits are well worthwhile, including...

- greater closeness to God
- spiritual strength for resisting temptation
- wisdom and love you need for guiding your family

The fact we can enjoy these kinds of blessings motivates me, by God's grace, to keep growing mature. I pray that is your desire as well!

*Father, when I'm tempted to cut corners or just give up, prompt me by Your Spirit with reminders of the tremendous blessings that come from spending time with You. Amen.*

# Calling on
# the Lord

When you read through the Bible, it becomes clear that men who desire God are men of prayer. For example, Abraham, throughout his life, built altars and called on the name of the Lord. Moses constantly prayed for direction as he led the nation of Israel. Solomon prayed for wisdom so he could judge the nation rightly. Nehemiah prayed for God's protection throughout the rebuilding of Jerusalem's wall. Paul prayed constantly for the churches where he had ministered.

If you've found it a challenge to pray regularly, you're not alone. It's easy to let the things of everyday life crowd out your time for prayer. You can change that by setting aside a specific time each day for meeting with God. Pick a time and stick with it—and you'll enjoy a more vibrant relationship with God.

*God, help me to establish a realistic and consistent habit of meeting with You in prayer. Thank You for reminding me that great men of God have always made prayer a priority. Amen.*

# God's Longings for Your Prayers

Have you ever felt inadequate about your prayer life? Have you wished you were better at prayer?

First, know that God isn't looking for polished prayers. What counts is having a transparent heart that communicates honestly and freely with Him. That said, however, it *is* possible to grow in prayer. Consider this: How did you become good at catching a ball, riding a bicycle, or mastering some other skill? You learned by doing. So it is with prayer—you learn to pray by praying.

The more you pray, the more of a comfortable habit it becomes. As with anything else, this takes time. Don't feel shy about praying. God longs to hear you. Come to Him often, and you'll feel more and more at ease in prayer.

*Father, I admit I'm still learning how to pray, and my faith is often weak. Strengthen me by Your Spirit so I can communicate with You more effectively. Amen.*

# Resting in God's Power

Do you have a problem today—a challenge you are facing, something at work you must resolve, an issue with your wife or a child or someone else? Then help yourself to God's power as promised in Philippians 4:13: "I can do all things through Christ who strengthens me."

This one mighty truth can give you the confidence you need for finding the right solution to a problem and carrying it out. And as you do, you'll want to make sure you express your gratitude to God in praise. Now, praise isn't an activity limited to life's positive moments—you can also thank God in the hard times. Looking to Him with praise even when life is rough will help you to maintain a right perspective no matter what happens.

> *God, please remind me of this promise often. When I doubt, help me to believe; when I am afraid, help me to trust in You. This is my confession today: You are my strength. Amen.*

# Everything
# You Need

The apostle Paul boldly declared, "God shall supply all your need according to His riches in glory by Christ Jesus" (Philippians 4:19). What a wonderful God we have! He promises to provide for all our needs, not *out* of His riches, but *according* to His riches. Do you see the difference? God gives in proportion to the immensity of His eternal wealth—that is, He gives generously.

You and I have much to praise God for as we experience His glorious provision day by day. If you ever find yourself wondering what to praise God for, consider what He has given you. This includes your spiritual blessings, both those you enjoy now and those awaiting you in heaven. As 2 Peter 1:3 says, "His divine power has given to us *all* things that pertain to life and godliness."

*Lord, Your resources are unlimited—the well will never run dry! You've given me all I need for life and godliness, and You'll supply my daily needs so I can accomplish Your will. Thank You!*

# Protection You Can Count On

Have you ever praised God for His protection in your life? Maybe you can recall specific times in the past when you've sensed God's protective care. It's also possible there have been times the Lord has shielded you from danger and you simply weren't aware of it.

David faced life-threatening dangers. Among them were the times that King Saul, David's predecessor to the throne, tried to kill him. Yet even in those circumstances David could pen this well-known verse: "Though I walk through the valley of the shadow of death, I will fear no evil; for You are with me" (Psalm 23:4). What peace is ours when we understand we are under God's protective hand! The next time you sense fear, remember that God protects you, and praise Him for His care.

*God, You have protected me and saved me from disaster more times than I will ever know. Thank You! Help me to live in the humble confidence that You are watching over me. Amen.*

# Making Worship a Priority

From the beginning of the church, believers have gathered to worship God through singing, studying the Word, and celebrating the Lord's resurrection. Among the reasons we need to participate in corporate worship is that it provides the only opportunity during the week for fellow believers to gather and hear God's Word taught and then reinforced through "exhorting one another" toward "love and good works" (Hebrews 10:24-25).

Because everyone in your family needs spiritual nourishment and stimulation, you must take leadership in making church attendance happen. It's *your* responsibility as a husband, father, and God-ordained leader of your family to nurture the spiritual needs of your wife and children. So look forward to Sunday with anticipation, and use the weekdays to prepare yourself and your family for worshiping God in His house, the church.

*God, so many good things happen when we join with other believers in worship. Help me to make this a priority for my family and to join wholeheartedly in the life of the church. Amen.*

# A Man of
# Your Word

I can't remember much about my wedding or what was said during the ceremony—it's all a blur in my mind. What about you? Since that day, have you thought back on the vows you made to your bride?

What's ironic about our tendency to forget about our vows is that they're among the most important words we've ever said. These promises were made not only before people, but before God. I'm sure you sincerely meant every promise you made to your bride on that day. What's important right now is for you to think about ways you can fulfill your vows daily. Won't you take a moment to pray and ask the Lord to help you recommit to carrying out those vows?

> *God, help me to be a man of my word and especially to follow through on the vows I made to my wife. Make me aware of opportunities to be the husband I promised to be. Amen.*

# A Noble
# Calling

God's call for husbands to love their wives is a noble calling—so much so, the Bible says we are to love our wives in the same way Christ loves the church. Jesus is our supreme example when it comes to how we demonstrate love, and the apostle Paul describes that love for us in Ephesians 5:22-33: It is sacrificial, purifying, nurturing, enduring, and active. So biblical love goes beyond mere words and emotions. It extends to our actions and includes a willingness to sacrifice one's self. In fact, Christ's love for the church was so great He was willing to die for her.

If you've felt inadequate about your ability to show such love, that's okay—humanly speaking, it's impossible to do. But with God's help, *all* things are possible. Ask, and He will gladly enable you.

*Jesus, today I ask for a miracle: Empower me to love my wife the way You love the church. I repent of selfishness. Renew my thinking when I face opportunities to sacrifice for my wife. Amen.*

# A Sacrificial Love

What are some ways you can actively show a Christlike love to your dear wife? Biblically speaking, love is willing to sacrifice one's self for the benefit of another. This may mean giving up your time, attention, or energy—going out of your way or enduring inconvenience.

One big way to do this is to take care of the kids. You could babysit them for a Saturday while your wife goes to a woman's seminar or retreat. Or you could make breakfast for the children so she can sleep in. Or you could watch the kids one evening a week so your wife can take a Bible class. Or what about hiring a babysitter and taking a class together? In all these ways you can give your wife a much-needed break... and build better relationships with your kids.

*God, sometimes the little sacrifices are the hardest to make! Help me to see small inconveniences as opportunities to be like You and to love my wife more effectively. Amen.*

# Encouraging
# Your Beloved

In Ephesians 5:29 we read that husbands are to nourish and cherish their wives, "just as the Lord does the church." What encouragement can you give to your wife today in the things of God and her spiritual advancement? In her efforts at managing the home? In her personal growth?

If you see opportunities for your wife to develop herself or her areas of giftedness, make it possible for her to take advantage of them. This might mean letting her take a class, giving her a book to read, or letting her get involved in a church group. It may require time and expense, but if it helps your wife to grow, then you and your family will benefit. Remember, this is what Christlike love is all about!

*Lord, You are constantly transforming and renewing our lives. Help me to cooperate with You and encourage my wife as You bless her with opportunities to mature and grow. Amen.*

# Keeping the
# Spark Aflame

When you were courting the woman who became your wife, did you strive to be her best friend? I'm sure you did! You enjoyed being in her company, and probably wanted to spend every waking moment together.

But after marriage, for some reason that thrill seems to fade away, doesn't it? The demands of everyday life have distracted you, and you haven't done what it takes to keep the spark of your relationship aflame.

How can you recapture the joy you knew while you were dating? Think back on those days. What did you do to nurture your relationship with your wife-to-be? Make a commitment now to do some of those activities again. After all, next to your relationship with God, your wife's friendship is the greatest treasure you possess.

> *Lord, I repent today for not always nurturing my friendship with my wife. Thank You for her, for the blessing of being married to her, and for the tremendous possibilities our relationship holds! Amen.*

# The Pleasure of Her Company

One way you can prove your love for your wife is by taking her out on a date each week—going out for dinner, going for a drive somewhere, doing something you both enjoy. Don't count the occasions when you're invited out or entertaining others. And don't let your children or work get in the way of a weekly opportunity to show your wife you still love her.

One date a week can mean a lot over the lifetime of a marriage. In 15 years that would mean 780 times spent together without interruptions and distractions. Don't you think that kind of alone time would make a difference in your relationship? The dates don't have to be elaborate or expensive. Just making time to enjoy each other's company is what counts.

*Jesus, You spent time with Your disciples and ministered to individuals. How could I not spend time alone with my lifelong partner and best friend? Help us enjoy simple dates on a regular basis. Amen.*

# The Art
# of Listening

I admit listening hasn't been one of my better qualities as a husband. I've had to work on this skill, and if the same is true for you, here are some suggestions I've found helpful:

- Realize that listening is an act of love. It says, "I value you and want to hear what you have to say."
- Make it a priority when you arrive home to spend a few minutes asking your wife about her day. Set aside all thoughts of work and give her your full attention.
- You know what it feels like when others don't listen to you. That's how your wife feels when you don't listen to her. So show her you care about her thoughts and feelings.

*Lord, You always listen when I call to You. Make me more like You—attentive to my wife's voice and concerned about whatever is on her heart. Open my ears, Lord! Amen.*

# God's Charge
# to Every Man

When a husband doesn't provide spiritual leadership in the home, it affects the spiritual well-being of the whole family. In fact, it's why we see Christian marriages and families deteriorating at an alarming rate these days.

Are you determined to keep that from happening in your home? All it takes is a willingness to pay the price. It means not being selfish, and living out the responsibilities God has given you.

If you are married, God has placed you in charge of your family's spiritual condition. Your growth affects theirs. While that's a scary thought, it's an exciting one as well. God is ready to help you. And when you have a positive impact on your family, that impact will spread beyond the walls of your home and into the world!

*Father, what a responsibility You've given me! And what a privilege! Empower me through Your Spirit to be a husband and father who glorifies You and blesses my family. Amen.*

# To Lead
# Is to Love

Did you know that when you provide spiritual leadership in your home, you are demonstrating your love for your wife and children? When you take the initiative to lead, you are showing love.

Yes, it takes work to lead. It means figuring out ways you can help your wife and children grow physically, mentally, and spiritually. It means providing the kind of environment that enables them to flourish. It means time and effort invested in their lives. This is what it means to fulfill your God-ordained role as the leader in the home. It all starts with love—if you love your family, you will take the time to lead. Don't ever give up—your family deserves your best effort, and God will reward you for your labors.

*Lord, do I reserve my best efforts for my work?*
*For my friends? For my hobbies? Help me to see*
*my family the way You do and to be a committed,*
*creative leader at home. Amen.*

# Equipping
# Yourself to Lead

The best way you can help lead your family is to make sure you are growing spiritually. This growth will give you the wisdom and strength you need for leading your wife and children. You can make this happen by...

- Reading the Bible daily so you are "complete, thoroughly equipped for every good work" (2 Timothy 3:17).
- Finding role models to emulate. "As iron sharpens iron, so one person sharpens another" (Proverbs 27:17 NIV).
- Avoiding negative influences. "Evil company corrupts good habits" (1 Corinthians 15:33).
- Avoiding tempting situations. "Flee... youthful lusts" (2 Timothy 2:22).
- Abiding in Christ so you can bear much fruit (John 15:1-8). This means praying to, depending upon, and actively obeying Christ.

*God, please transform my family by transforming me. Speak to me through Your Word, through Your Spirit, and through godly men. Make me the husband and father my family needs. Amen.*

# The Real Thing

Can your children tell, by your words and actions, that God's Word has an effect on you?

Kids can quickly tell the difference between what is authentic and what isn't. If your life reveals you don't take God seriously, your children will notice—and they will probably conclude they have little reason to take the Lord seriously either.

How you conduct yourself has a very real impact on your children. That's why Ephesians 4:1 urges you to "live a life worthy of the calling you have received" (NIV). People are watching you—especially your kids. When they see you love God and desire to obey Him, they will realize your faith is for real. They will see God and His Word in a positive light. And that will encourage them to seek and follow the Lord in their own lives.

*God, I want to be the real deal spiritually—for Your glory, for my own good, and so my kids can have a good example to follow. Thank You for my kids…they keep me honest! Amen.*

# A Key to
# Successful Parenting

How you care for your wife is a major factor in caring for your children. Why? Because parenting is a partnership.

As you love your wife, you'll build her sense of well-being. This, in turn, enables her to better focus her attention on your children and have a positive influence on them. So by loving your wife, you are having an impact on your kids. That's one way parenting is a partnership.

When you work as partners, the task of raising children becomes much easier. So as you consider your responsibilities as a dad, remember that a key to your success is your love for your wife. Take a moment now to offer up a prayer of thanks for her, and make sure you affirm her daily as she helps you in the nurture of your family.

*Lord, thank You for the partner You have given me. How can I be a better partner for her? Bless her today with strength and wisdom and joy and a sensitive, caring husband. Amen.*

# It's the Heart
# that Matters

A child's behavior is driven by what is in his or her heart. That is, all behavior begins in the heart, whether good or bad. So all the training and discipline you give to your children needs to be directed to their hearts. When you shape their hearts, then you will shape their behavior as well.

Your children are given to you by God, and their hearts are your stewardship from Him. He expects you to do your part in raising them to know and love Him.

As you interact with your children, are you making a conscious effort to shepherd their hearts? Are you seeking to shape their inner person and not just their outer behavior? Focus on molding their hearts, and you'll influence their thoughts, words, and deeds.

*Heavenly Father, I confess that I underestimate my influence on my kids' hearts. Help me to see how much my words and actions shape them. What a responsibility! Lead me, Lord, for their sake. Amen.*

# Raising Up
# Godly Kids

When it comes to influencing your children, here are the absolute essentials for every dad:

- *Love your wife*—When you love your children's mother, you love them as well.
- *Take your family to church*—This simple act is a giant step toward assuming spiritual leadership in your home.
- *Grow spiritually*—This is the only way you'll gain the wisdom and strength you need for parenting.
- *Spend time with your children*—Close relationships come only with time.
- *Model Christlike behavior*—Then you can say to your children, "Imitate me, just as I also imitate Christ" (1 Corinthians 11:1).

*Lord, these things seem so simple, but You can use them to shape my kids' lives. May the things I say and do produce good fruit in them as they begin their own relationships with You. Amen.*

# When You're Overwhelmed

Are you feeling overwhelmed as a father? Maybe you feel inadequate for the task of parenting. Perhaps your children don't always cooperate with you. Or you've fallen short in your spiritual growth and you fear you're not the best example for them.

Whatever it is that discourages you, don't give up. God wants you to depend on Him for help. That's why the Bible says, "Cast all your anxiety on him because he cares for you" (1 Peter 5:7 NIV). And it's why we're told, "Trust in the LORD with all your heart, and lean not on your own understanding; in all your ways acknowledge Him, and He shall direct your paths" (Proverbs 3:5-6).

Give your concerns to God. Lean on Him and trust Him, and He will show you the way.

> *Heavenly Father, my kids need a better dad—one who loves wholeheartedly and serves sacrificially. Make me that kind of dad today. Cleanse my heart and renew my mind. Amen.*

# Making the Time

One of the greater challenges of fatherhood is finding time to spend with the kids. Most families are busy, and yours is no exception. However, busyness is not an excuse for failing to set aside time for your children. If something is important to you, somehow you'll find a way to make it happen, right?

So where do you fit your together times into an already-busy schedule? If you're like most families, breakfast or dinnertime are two key possibilities. Getting the time established might be hard. But once it's set and you're committed, you'll find it easier to make it happen. Don't betray your children through neglect. Be available to them. Outside of God and your wife, they're the most important priorities in your life.

*Heavenly Father, have I neglected my kids? Help me to establish fun, meaningful, and regular times to connect with them. May my schedule be an accurate reflection of my priorities. Amen.*

# Consistency Counts

Through the years I've talked with many ministry leaders, including those on college campuses like UCLA. Frequently I ask them which students are the most difficult to reach for Jesus Christ. Without exception they have reported it is the children of nominal Christian parents. It seems the students from such homes wanted nothing to do with a faith that hadn't been lived out in their family.

This confirms that the greatest influence you can have on your children will come from your Christian example at home. The reality of Christ is nowhere better demonstrated than in your consistent, godly conduct. By contrast, inconsistency breeds confusion. So ask God to help you remain steadfast...for the sake of your children and their spiritual well-being.

*Lord, the last thing I want to be is a lukewarm, compromising Christian. Today I renew my commitment to live in wholehearted devotion to You. Help me to live with purpose and passion. Amen.*

# Effective Discipline
## Starts with Love

Did you know that when God disciplines us, it is a sign of His love for us? Proverbs 3:12 says, "Whom the LORD loves He corrects, just as a father the son in whom he delights." And Hebrews 12:6 says, "Whom the LORD loves He chastens."

Because God is perfectly just and wise, we can know His discipline is consistent and fair. And the discipline we administer to our children should be the same.

Kids usually don't like discipline when it's given. But if you make sure it's appropriate, explain the reason for it, and back it up with affirmations of your love, your children will eventually realize you have their best interests at heart. Those are the keys to effective and successful discipline.

*Lord, I know You want what's best for me. May my children be just as sure that I want what's best for them. Each time I discipline my children, may our relationship grow stronger. Amen.*

# Think Before You Discipline

Sometimes in our zeal to discipline our children we can end up reacting to their wrong behavior in a harsh or inconsistent manner. If we're not careful, in our efforts to set things right, we can do more harm than good. The apostle Paul cautions: "Fathers, do not provoke your children, lest they become discouraged" (Colossians 3:21). To "provoke" means to make angry, and to "become discouraged" speaks of losing heart.

If you're too severe in your discipline, you can end up crushing your children's spirits, and they'll withdraw from you—until one day, when they are old enough, they'll just walk away. So when it comes time to chastise, make sure the punishment is appropriate and consistent. Avoid angering or goading your kids to the point they give up hope of ever pleasing you.

*Heavenly Father, keep me from ever disciplining my children in anger. When I discipline them, empower me to use loving words and actions so they know how much I love them. Amen.*

# A Team Effort

Earlier I said that parenting is a partnership. That's especially true when it comes to discipline!

It's important that you and your wife agree on *how, when, where,* and *why* you correct your children. You need to determine beforehand how you are going to deal with different types of wrong behavior. I'm sure you've already noticed that no two children are alike. Each child needs to be disciplined differently, and yet at the same time you need to maintain consistency. That's why it helps to plan ahead.

Another great benefit of making these decisions in advance is it helps your kids to know the ground rules—what makes for acceptable behavior, and what doesn't. This knowledge will encourage better behavior and greater harmony in your home.

> *God, lead my wife and me as we talk about this issue. Help us to give our children clear boundaries, enforce those boundaries fairly, and express our love consistently. Amen.*

# Work Is a
# Good Thing

Rumor has it that work is a consequence of man's fall into sin. But work existed before Adam and Eve sinned. In Genesis 1, we see God at work creating the heavens and earth. And when God was finished, He *rested from all His work* (Genesis 2:3). We also read that God placed Adam "in the garden of Eden to tend and keep it" (2:15). So God modeled for us the inherent dignity of work. Then He assigned man, made in His image, to work in the garden. So work is a good thing. It was created by God, and through it we are blessed to be able to provide for our families and contribute to society. What are some other benefits of work that you can thank God for right now?

> *Jesus, You said Your Father gave You work to do. I believe my work is part of Your plan for my life too, so I embrace it wholeheartedly. Thank You for the privilege of working. Amen.*

# The Profit
# of Work

Have you ever noticed that our physical and mental makeup thrives on work? We derive great satisfaction from a job well done. That's because God created us to be workers. In fact, the Bible repeatedly affirms the value and importance of work. For example, in Proverbs 12:11 we read, "Those who work their land will have abundant food" (NIV). Proverbs 14:23 says, "All hard work brings a profit, but mere talk leads only to poverty" (NIV). And the New Testament proclaims, "If anyone will not work, neither shall he eat" (2 Thessalonians 3:10).

God knows what is best for you. He ordained that you be productive through work. That should help you to have a positive attitude toward your job, which, in turn, can have a positive effect on all your co-workers.

*God, help me to approach my work with enthusiasm and energy. May my commitment to be a good employee be a blessing to my company, my supervisor, and my co-workers. Amen.*

# Representing Christ on the Job

At your workplace, do you see yourself as Christ's ambassador? An ambassador is one who represents another—for example, the word is used to speak of a representative from one country to another. So being an ambassador for Christ means properly representing Him in whatever you do, including at work. You represent God as you go about doing your job.

What kind of ambassador are you? Matthew 5:14, 16 says, "You are the light of the world...Let your light so shine before men, that they may see your good works and glorify your Father in heaven." No matter how difficult or challenging your workload or workplace environment, every day is an exciting new opportunity to give the people around you a positive representation of God and the Christian life.

*God, help me to see myself as Your ambassador to my workplace. May I represent You well—by humbly serving others and by performing my assigned tasks with excellence and joy. Amen.*

# The Source of
Contentment

Are you feeling content about your job? Maybe your answer is no because you work with difficult people, or you've been treated unfairly, or you feel overdue for a pay raise.

But you *can* know contentment at work even when things are rough. When Paul said, "I have learned to be content whatever the circumstances" (Philippians 4:11 NIV), he was in prison at the time, possibly facing execution. Yet he was content. Why? His contentment wasn't based on *circumstances*, but on the *Person of Christ*. Paul wrote, "My God shall supply all your need according to His riches in glory by Christ Jesus" (Philippians 4:19). When you focus on how God has met your needs instead of on your circumstances, contentment is possible, even in a difficult job.

> *God, when I am discontent, help me not to blame others. Instead, show me how I can find contentment in You and let the joy of knowing You affect every area of my life. Amen.*

# Working unto
# the Lord

If you are discontent with your job, you'll find it helpful to ask yourself these questions:

*Why am I here?* If you see your job as God's calling, you'll view it as a ministry opportunity.

*For whom am I working?* When you see yourself as working for God, you are free to serve others no matter how unreasonable or thankless they are.

*With whom am I working?* Every person at your workplace is an eternal soul who needs Christ. That makes your job a mission field.

*What am I working for?* Money? Prestige? Power? If you are working for any of these, you will never be content. Only when you work for God's glory will you know contentment.

> *Father, help me to answer these questions honestly. Where my thinking is distorted, renew my mind so I can think about my job the way You do. Amen.*

# The Power
# of Integrity

Are you a model of excellence in the workplace? One key element of excellence is the character quality of integrity. *Integrity* is defined as being of sound moral principle, upright, honest, and sincere. Of all the people in the workforce, we as men of God should possess integrity. This trait should be the hallmark of our business life. Others should not be able to accuse us of dishonest business practices. Instead, like Daniel in the Old Testament, we should be found "trustworthy and neither corrupt nor negligent" (Daniel 6:4 NIV).

When people know they can trust you, you're likely to be given greater responsibilities. And even if that doesn't happen, you've achieved an even more important goal: You've given unbelievers the opportunity to view God and Christianity in a positive light.

*Lord, do others see me as a man of integrity? Or have I compartmentalized my life, acting one way at church and another way at work? Help me to please You in all I do. Amen.*

# A Passion
# That's Contagious

How impassioned are you about your work? Do you approach each workday with an...

- eagerness to model Christ before a watching world?
- eagerness to contribute your energies to the success of your company or business?
- eagerness to contribute one more day's wages to the well-being of your family?
- eagerness to declare the praises of Him who called you out of darkness into His wonderful light?

When you're impassioned about your work, it lifts up others and contributes to a better workplace environment. And, of course, God will be glorified, which is your whole reason for being.

*God, You have given me plenty of reasons to live with passion! When my energy is low and my work is uninspired, remind me of my high calling and the riches of Your empowering grace. Amen.*

# Loving the Church
## as God Does

The apostle Paul wrote more books in the New Testament than any other writer. And aside from his consistent theme of salvation by grace through faith, his teachings on the church are one of the most dominant topics he addressed. That should serve as a clue that the church is an important subject. If God inspired Paul to say so much about the church, then clearly it is important to Him. So it should be important to you too.

As a believer, you are a member of Christ's body, the church (Ephesians 5:30). On a scale of 1-10, how much of a priority is church to you? What do your attendance, giving, prayers, and service reveal about the place the church has in your life?

> *Lord, thank You for reminding me how important the church is to You. I want it to be important to me too! Guide me as I reassess my relationship with the church today. Amen.*

# Active
## Versus Passive

For many years I lived a lukewarm form of Christianity with little or no involvement in a local church. Call it drifting, call it distraction, or even sin. My heart was not consumed with the things of the Lord. Then a dynamic Christian man ignited in me a new passion for God, His Word, and the church. I began to grow, and the results were life-changing not only for me but also my family. We gained many new friends who cared for and helped us, and now we're actively engaged in serving others.

Church can do that for your family too. Christ is calling for you to be active. Developing a passion for the church is a matter of obedience, which leads to many blessings. So determine to have a passion for the church!

*Lord, thank You for reminding me that a lackadaisical attitude about the church is sinful. I want to be passionate about the church because I want to be passionate about You. Help me, Lord. Amen.*

# Worshiping God Together

If worshiping God and growing spiritually are priorities in your life, you will attend church faithfully on Sunday. You'll also take advantage of other opportunities for spiritual input, such as classes or seminars for men or couples.

You and your family can never get too much input from God's Word! A wise man seeks wisdom (Proverbs 15:14), and that wisdom is available at your local church. Do you want to be a better spiritual leader for your family? The mere act of faithfully attending church with your wife and kids will go a long way toward making that happen. Your family will benefit as you grow more mature in the faith, and you will enjoy the fruit of their spiritual growth as well.

*God, sometimes "becoming a spiritual leader" sounds like a lofty, nebulous goal. But faithfully taking my family to church—I can do that! Help me to take this practical step toward spiritual maturity. Amen.*

# Riches
# for Eternity

In the Bible, Jesus spoke frequently about money. Why? Not because the God who created all things needs our resources—it all came from Him anyway! But because we need to exercise care over our heart attitude toward money, which can easily distract us from the real priorities in life.

It's been said you can tell a man's priorities by looking at his checkbook. When you invest your treasure in God's church and people, that's evidence you have a true interest in the well-being of others. As Matthew 6:21 says, "Where your treasure is, there your heart will be also." Do your expenditures reveal where your treasures are? If they are in heaven, then you are laying up riches that will last for all eternity.

*Lord, You know my heart better than I do. Thank You for reminding me that the way I spend my money actually shapes my heart. Help me to make eternal investments with my money. Amen.*

# A Cheerful Giver

If you haven't established a pattern of giving regularly to the church, you can start the same way Elizabeth and I did. We started with what we had, which wasn't much! And we began giving to the church from the front end of each paycheck instead of the back end. That communicated to God that He was our priority.

Have you asked God to help you handle your money with discernment? Ask Him to reveal any areas of greed or selfishness in your life. Your goal is to give with a cheerful heart. As Paul wrote, "He who sows sparingly will also reap sparingly, and he who sows bountifully will also reap bountifully…for God loves a cheerful giver" (2 Corinthians 9:6-7).

> *God, I've heard this phrase a lot, but today I wonder—am I a cheerful giver? All I have is Yours, and You will supply all I need, so I choose to give with a cheerful heart! Amen.*

# We All Need
# Each Other

At the time of your salvation, God gave you spiritual gifts. These are special abilities given by God and empowered by the Holy Spirit for the purpose of ministering to others in the church. God wants to work through you for the good of others (1 Corinthians 12:7,11).

Now, you can't mail or phone in the use of your spiritual gifts. And you can't delegate them. You must be physically involved for your gifts to be any use. Can you imagine what a church would be like if every member made use of his or her spiritual gifts? It would be a bit of heaven on earth. And it would be a powerful testimony to a watching world, which would see Jesus Christ through our actions.

*Lord, I'm not very bold about putting my spiritual gifts to work, but today You're reminding me that I can make a difference in people's lives. I'm ready, Lord—show me the way. Amen.*

# Living to
# Bless Others

When it comes to spiritual gifts, you are unique. Your spiritual abilities are an inherent part of your Christian makeup, and your giftedness is not like anyone else's.

That you are one of a kind affirms just how important it is for you to have an active part in church life. As Paul explains in 1 Corinthians 12, every part of the body of Christ has a vital role. There are no greater or lesser gifts (verses 15-27). So when any one person—including you—is absent, it's felt by the rest of the body.

What are some ways you've been blessed by the spiritual giftedness of others in your church? Thank God for the benefits you've enjoyed as a result of the Spirit's work.

> *God, thank You for the way You've blessed me through other people in the church. Help me to never take their influence for granted. And help me remember to thank them too. Amen.*

# A Right
# Perspective

When you are using your God-given gifts, others will be blessed. And you will feel blessed as you obediently and humbly minister your gifts. Yours will be the joy of knowing that you are fulfilling your special role in the proper functioning of Christ's body, the church.

At times you might feel like you're not having much impact. When that happens, remember this: All God asks is that you serve faithfully (1 Corinthians 4:2). It's not the size of your ministry that counts. Rather, it's your availability to God. As you let the Lord work through you, the Holy Spirit will make things happen. He will bear spiritual fruit. And one day, you will receive the ultimate reward—hearing Christ say, "Well done, good and faithful servant."

*Jesus, when I don't see many results from my service, help me to remember that I'm ultimately serving You and that You will one day reward every good deed. Amen.*

# Being a
# True Friend

One way you can "earn the right" to share about your faith in Christ is by having true concern for others. You may have heard the saying, "People don't care what you know until they know that you care." That's very true—your fellow workers, neighbors, and others must see you as approachable, caring, and friendly.

Before you can expect people to listen to what you might say about Christ, you need to build friendships with them. And as you become a better neighbor, you will earn the right to be heard.

It all starts with genuine caring. Show a real interest in what's happening in other people's lives. This will enable you to pray for them, know their needs, and be a true friend.

*Jesus, You, the Creator of the universe, call us Your friends. Help me to pay attention to people and to notice when someone needs a friend. Amen.*

# Loving the Unlovely

It's easy to show love to attractive or successful people. But Jesus commands us to love the unlovely, and even those who hate us (Matthew 5:44). Years ago, someone in our home Bible study invited a non-Christian woman from his workplace and, to his surprise, she came. This woman did not take care of herself—her hair was messy, her clothes dirty. Though she was unlovely, everyone endeavored to show love and care for her. She continued to attend, and in time, she accepted Christ! It would have been easy to ignore her because of her appearance. But we're called to love the unlovely, and let God do His incredible, life-changing work in them. We are to view each person for what he or she really is—a lost soul in need of a Savior.

*Lord, help me to look past people's outward appearance and to see their true worth, their dignity, and their need. You can meet those needs— sometimes through me. Amen.*

# Temporary Sacrifices, Eternal Fruit

How much are you willing to sacrifice to show friendship or concern to an unbeliever? It may mean having lunch with an acquaintance and listening to him pour out his heart (a sacrifice of time). It may mean inviting a fellow worker to a ball game and paying for the tickets (a sacrifice of money). It may mean inviting your neighbors over for a meal or dessert (a sacrifice of time and money).

Whatever the sacrifice, whether small or large, it will be worthwhile. How much is a soul worth? It cost God the death of His only Son on the cross. What's a few dollars or a little time in relation to eternity? Be willing to sacrifice yourself—God did!

*Jesus, when I consider what You sacrificed for me, I can feel more thankful for opportunities to sacrifice for others. Thank You for the privilege of following in Your footsteps. Amen.*

# Living as
# Good Samaritans

Some Christians have the mistaken idea that unbelievers are "the enemy." As a result, they have little or nothing to do with them.

In the story of the Good Samaritan (Luke 10:30-37), the Samaritan did not see the wounded Jew as his enemy, even though the Jews of that day were hostile toward Samaritans. Rather, the robbers were the enemy, and the wounded Jew was a victim. We rightly view victims of tragedy with empathy and concern. So why don't we view the unbelievers around us in the same way? They are the victims of Satan and sin (2 Timothy 2:26), and they can't help themselves (Romans 3:10-18).

Pray for unbelievers and show you care for them. Take every opportunity to be their friend and neighbor.

*Jesus, have I passed by any victims lately? Open my eyes and show me someone today who needs my prayers, my time, my caring attention. Keep me from labeling victims as enemies. Amen.*

# A Willingness
# to Share

Men often tell me they don't know how to share their faith, or say they don't know their Bible well enough to talk to others about it. For these reasons, they shy away from opportunities for reaching others for Christ.

But it's not necessary for you to be an expert before you can let others know about the most significant aspect of your life. You already know better than anyone how you became a Christian, and how taking that step changed your life. All you need is to be willing to speak. God will do the rest, for it is His Holy Spirit that works in people's hearts.

*Lord, the first step is always the hardest. Please help me notice opportunities to talk about what You have done in my life. And may my words always be filled with grace. Amen.*

# Proclaiming
# God's Goodness

I don't know how long you've been a Christian, but you may have heard other believers talk about sharing your testimony, or your story of how you became a Christian. Even a new believer can do this, according to Mark 5:1-20. There we read about a man tormented by demons. Jesus cast out the demons, and the man was so thrilled he asked if he could follow Jesus. Our Lord didn't say, "Sure, sit at My feet and let Me tutor you for a few years until you are ready to share your testimony." Instead, He said, "Go home to your friends, and tell them what great things the Lord has done for you" (5:19). As a new believer, the man had all he needed to testify of his experience with Jesus. The same is true for you. Are you willing?

> *God, You have done some incredible things in my life, and I have no reason to be embarrassed to talk about them. Guide my speech, and use my words to help others know You. Amen.*

# The Bare
# Essentials

Your personal testimony can be broken down into three parts:

1. What my life was like before I met Jesus.
2. How I met Jesus.
3. What my life has been like since meeting Jesus.

Think back over the circumstances that led to your salvation, and the changes you've experienced since. Write out what happened to you. Once you've done this, you're ready "to give an answer to everyone who asks you to give the reason for the hope that you have" (1 Peter 3:15 NIV). Take a moment now to pray and thank God for your salvation. Then ask Him to give you an opportunity this week to share with someone else the reason for your hope.

*Lord, thank You for giving me a story to share. As I look back on the way You've changed my life, help me talk about my story in a way that leads others to You. Amen.*

# Building Bridges

Become a caring neighbor. Develop friendships. Build bridges. *This* is what it means to develop a heart for reaching others. You don't need to be a pastor or Bible scholar to share your faith. But you do need to earn the right to be heard by those around you.

What are some ways you can build bridges that will help transport the message of Christ from your heart to the hearts of others? As you endeavor to live your life for Christ, others will see His transforming work in you through your positive attitude, pursuit of integrity, edifying speech, good work ethic, faithful church involvement, and a strong love for and commitment to your family. These can help open the door for you to build connections that eventually allow you to share about Jesus.

*Jesus, "sharing my faith" sounds scary. Being a caring neighbor or a friend—I can do that. Make me more like You, so that when I'm around others, they want to learn more about You. Amen.*

# God Will
# Do the Work

Whenever you feel inadequate about reaching out to unbelievers, remember: Salvation is *God's* job. Building bridges is *your* job. And so is prayer. As you connect with people, you can pray for God to walk across those bridges into the hearts and lives of relatives, workmates, and neighbors. Pray for opportunities to communicate (Colossians 4:3), and pray for God to override your fears and give you boldness (Ephesians 6:19).

Are there people you can think of now whom you ought to pray for? Put their names on a list and pray for them regularly. Build bridges by showing you care for them. The time for sharing Christ might not come for a while—even a few years. But if you're consistent in prayer, you'll be ready when the door opens up.

*God, guide my thoughts now as I consider who to be praying for. Give me strength to keep praying through the months and years if necessary. Thank You for answering prayer! Amen.*

# Points of
# Interaction

You can build bridges with unbelievers in a number of ways. One is to invite non-Christians to join you in your hobbies and interests. This allows you to have a point of common interest. You can also "meet unbelievers in the middle." What do I mean by that? You will find very few non-Christians in your church. For the most part, you'll encounter them in your neighborhood, your workplace, at the Little League field. Get to know people where they live and play. You could even become a coach for your child's soccer team or join an adult sports league. Both will allow unbelievers to see a Christian in action. Doing volunteer work in the community is yet another way you can serve as salt and light for the gospel. Can you think of additional ways to build bridges?

> *Jesus, You moved freely among people who were rejected by those who considered themselves religious. You loved them and blessed them...please help me to do the same. Amen.*

# Resisting Temptation

Of all the questions men ask me, most deal with the matter of purity. Today's culture has made it hard for Christian men to think pure thoughts and develop pure habits. But this problem isn't new—temptation has been around since the beginning of history. In fact, God faced these same issues firsthand in the person of His Son, Jesus Christ (Hebrews 2:17-18). And we're told victory is possible: "How can a young man cleanse his way? By taking heed according to Your word...Your word I have hidden in my heart, that I might not sin against You" (Psalm 119:9,11). Victory is yours when you heed God and His Word. Spend time in the Bible and hide it in your heart, and you'll have the resources to resist temptation and stay pure.

*Lord, when impure thoughts try to gain access to my mind, help me to fill my mind with Your Word. Lead me to passages I can memorize and call on when I need to. Amen.*

# The Real Key
## to Success

When you spend time in God's Word and grow spiritually, you are equipping yourself to make wise and godly decisions in all that you do. Joshua, who was Moses' successor, understood the importance of making good decisions. God told Joshua, "This Book of the Law shall not depart from your mouth, but you shall meditate in it day and night, that you may observe to do according to all that is written in it. For then you will make your way prosperous, and then you will have good success" (Joshua 1:8). Did you notice the key to real success? It's all about following and obeying God's Word. When your decisions line up with Scripture, God will honor you and bring blessing into your life.

*God, whenever I think about prosperity and success, may I remember this verse. Remind me that blessing and obedience to Your Word go hand in hand. Amen.*

# The Right
# Kind of Resolve

It's tough to make a decision that's unpopular, but Joshua wasn't afraid to do so. The first time the Jewish people had the opportunity to enter the Promised Land, Moses picked 12 spies to check it out. When they returned, Joshua and Caleb urged taking possession of the land (Numbers 14:6-8). But all the other spies lamented, "We are not able to go up against the people, for they are stronger than we" (Numbers 13:31). Joshua and Caleb were overruled, and God punished the Israelites for their lack of faith.

After his many years of service to Israel, Joshua told the people, "Choose for yourselves this day whom you will serve...as for me and my house, we will serve the LORD" (Joshua 24:15). Do you have the same kind of uncompromising resolve in your life?

*Lord, help me to see what I'm really serving—
money, popularity, myself...or You. Serving You
is such a privilege! Please show me opportunities
to be Your servant today. Amen.*

# Sowing
# Good Seed

There's a quip that says, "If you don't like what you are reaping, change what you are sowing." If you find yourself disappointed or frustrated with life in general, then maybe you need to take a closer look at what you're sowing. Are you preoccupied with personal ambitions and self-gratification? Or are you focused outward upon God and the people around you?

God designed for Christians to experience satisfaction by pursuing Him and giving themselves in service to others. Romans 12:10-11 says we're to "be kindly affectionate to one another with brotherly love, in honor giving preference to one another... serving the Lord." When you sow love toward God and others, you will reap blessings. In fact, God will bless "exceedingly abundantly above all that we ask or think"! (Ephesians 3:20).

> God, I don't often think about the kind of seed I'm sowing. Thank You for reminding me to sow good seed by humbly serving others. Guide me in Your steps today. Amen.

# Marriage
# God's Way

Marriage is a great invention of God. And a marriage where the husband loves his wife as Christ loved the church is a true witness to the reality of the Christian faith. But a marriage that honors Jesus Christ is not easy to come by. If you want this kind of marriage, you'll have to work at it.

God wants to bless you and your marriage. And He will, when you follow His blueprint for this sacred relationship. It requires having a heart yielded to Him. It requires a willingness to grow spiritually, which means spending time in the Bible so you can make wiser decisions and provide spiritual leadership. And it requires a sacrificial love for your wife. Yes, that's all work...but oh, the blessings that await you when you do marriage God's way!

*Lord, today I affirm that a good marriage is worth the effort. Bless my wife and me as we invest our time, energy, and money into building a relationship that honors You. Amen.*

# The Marriage Team

All through my growing-up years, I loved sports so much that I played in a lot of sandlot-type events. The teams were always organized on the spot, and winning generally depended on which team ended up with the best athletes. But sometimes when a bunch of average guys played well as a team, they would experience victory over the more athletic group.

This principle about winning as a team is true in marriage: Marriage works best when a husband and wife work in harmony. That's the way God designed this special relationship. And when you follow God's plan for working together as a couple, your marriage will be a little bit of heaven on earth. What are some ways you can become more of a team player in your interactions with your wife today?

*Lord, I admit that I'm not always a great team player at home. Today I choose to follow Your direction as You show me ways I can be a better partner in our marriage. Amen.*

# God's
# Ideal Design

God created marriage. In Genesis 2:18 He said, "It is not good that man should be alone; I will make him a helper comparable to him." After the Lord created Eve, He then said, "A man shall leave his father and mother and be joined to his wife, and they shall become one flesh." In His perfect wisdom, God designed man and woman to complement each other and to enjoy a permanent and complete union with each other.

Whenever you take the time to nurture that oneness, you bring honor to God and acknowledge His ideal design. As you love your wife, you are showing love and obedience to God as well. And as a result, you'll experience the fullness and blessings that God designed for a married couple to enjoy.

*God, "nurturing oneness" with my wife isn't something I think about every day. Help me to make that a priority from now on, and please show me creative ways to show her my love. Amen.*

# Real
# Oneness

What happens when you work as a team to fulfill God's plan for your marriage?

*You'll bring honor to God*—The harmony and beauty in your unity will proclaim to the world the wisdom of God's plan for marriage, thus bringing honor to Him.

*You'll bring honor to your marriage*—A watching world will see your oneness and will want to follow your godly example.

*You'll experience completeness*—God's plan requires a husband and wife to work together, with each enhancing the other. As you each contribute your strengths and skills for the good of the marriage, you'll know true oneness. You'll feel complete as a couple!

*God, You've given my wife and me a lot of good reasons to work together to follow Your plan for our marriage. Please remind me of these three whenever I think and act selfishly. Amen.*

# Praying as
# a Couple

Not only does prayer makes a big difference in life, it also does the same in a marriage. Making time to lift your hearts together to God will take both your prayers and your relationship up another level. So carve out a time each day when you can go to the Lord in mutual prayer. It doesn't have to be long—even just a few minutes is good.

Praying as a couple knits your hearts together for common spiritual concerns and direction. Your wife will hear your heart as you talk to God, and you will do likewise as you listen to her prayers. As you continue to make this a habit, you'll find your desires becoming more and more fused together, bringing you closer as husband and wife.

*Lord, You taught Your disciples how to pray simple, heartfelt prayers. Help my wife and me to keep it simple and to share our thoughts and concerns with You—together. Amen.*

# Swift
# to Hear

Listening is a lost art. Too often we're impatient with others. We fail to respect people long enough to let them finish speaking before we jump in. We tend to value what we want to say more than what others have to say.

This problem is common in marriages. We become so used to each other that we don't listen as carefully as we should. We are so absorbed with our own thoughts or pursuits that we don't really pay attention to our spouse.

Do you remember how much you enjoyed listening to your wife when you first fell in love? Think upon your most recent conversations. Do you need to rekindle your listening skills? Do as James 1:19 says, and "be swift to hear, slow to speak."

*God, do I interrupt my wife? Do I really take her words to heart? Help me to value my wife's words, to cherish her thoughts and feelings, and to show her how much I care. Amen.*

# Speaking
# with Grace

When Elizabeth and I were first married, there were two topics we couldn't discuss without getting into an argument—religion and politics. Then, miracle of miracles, God came into our marriage and religion was the only thing we wanted to talk about!

Are there topics you and your wife avoid because they cause arguments to erupt? Together, identify those hot buttons right now and determine that, with God's help, you won't raise your voices or get angry when those matters arise. Colossians 3:19 says, "Husbands, love your wives and do not be harsh with them" (NIV). So commit to being a peacemaker. As Proverbs 15:1 says, "A soft answer turns away wrath." Bottom line? Speak with grace. *How* you speak is often more important than *what* you say.

> *God, I pray that today You will help me to value my wife's opinion. And when it's my turn to talk, may my wife always hear these words in the background: "I love you." Amen.*

# Practicing
# Forgiveness

Whenever there's an argument between you and your wife, be quick to ask for forgiveness. Be willing to be the first to say, "I'm sorry." Rather than be a part of the problem, practice "sweetness of the lips" (Proverbs 16:21).

Now, some people assume that asking for forgiveness is the same thing as admitting you're wrong. But that's not true. Seeking forgiveness is not an issue of who is right or wrong. Rather, it's an issue of obeying God. Jesus said, "If you bring your gift to the altar, and there remember that your brother has something against you, leave your gift there before the altar, and go...First be reconciled to your brother" (Matthew 5:23-24). It is the wise husband who is willing to calmly settle or end an argument by asking for forgiveness.

> *Lord, please remind me every day of the difference between winning an argument and building a relationship. I know which is most important, but I need Your help to act accordingly. Amen.*

# Your Wife,
# Your Friend

How would you define intimacy? If you're like most men (including yours truly), you will probably think in terms of sexual intimacy or lovemaking. While that is a part of intimacy, there's more to the definition. It also refers to great closeness—the kind that the closest of friends share, in which they feel they can talk about anything.

Are you enjoying that kind of friendship with your wife? Sometimes the friendship part of marriages goes through a dry spell, but this doesn't need to last. Purpose in your heart to cultivate *both* friendship and marital intimacy with your wife. Build the kind of relationship where she can say of you, "This is my beloved, and this is my friend" (Song of Solomon 5:16).

*God, You can make all things new—including my friendship with my wife. As You renew us individually day by day, may our relationship also experience new life as we follow You. Amen.*

# Where
# Intimacy Starts

Every good marriage must, at heart, be a friendship between two people who truly care about each other. You as a husband must think as much of your wife as you think of any good friend, and even more so because you are life partners.

When you have that kind of close friendship in place, you'll find it naturally encourages a close physical relationship that fulfills each other sexually. In other words, intimate passion starts with the fuel of a faithful friendship, mutual respect, and clear communication. I once heard a speaker say, "If you want to have sex with your wife, be willing to go to the mall with her." When you are good friends, you'll enjoy a more intimate sex life.

*God, help me to love my wife consistently—in our work, our play, our conversations, and our lovemaking. Help me to communicate my love for my wife in all I do. Amen.*

# How Talking
# Can Help

My personal opinion as to why sexual intimacy is such a problem for many married couples is a failure for the husband or wife (or both) to give careful consideration to the fact men and women are wired differently, and that is true when it comes to physical intimacy. When we overlook or refuse to accept male-female distinctives, we begin to develop faulty reasoning like, *My wife should respond the same way as I do when it comes to sex.* Then when she doesn't, we wonder, *What's wrong with her?*…and…well, you know the rest.

This brings us back to the importance of communication. The best way to better understand your differences is to talk. Doing this will definitely help your marriage!

> *Lord, I confess that I haven't instigated many conversations with my wife about our physical relationship. How can I help her feel safe enough to share her feelings with me? Guide me, I pray. Amen.*

# Equal
# Yet Different

As Christians, you and your wife are equals before God. Galatians 3:28 says that from a spiritual standpoint, "there is neither male nor female; for you are all one in Christ Jesus." But when it comes to anatomy and physiology, God wired men and women differently because of the distinct roles He designed for them in marriage and the family. The man is to give strong, protective leadership, and the woman is to support and sustain life and living. These roles are taught in Scripture, and when we honor them, we will know completeness in the marital relationship.

Are you treating your wife as a spiritual equal? And at the same time encouraging her womanly distinctives? When you do both, you'll help her be all God designed her to be.

*Lord, there is no one like my wife. Help me to cherish and nurture her tremendous gifts and wonderful distinctives. May I empower her to become the person You created her to be. Amen.*

# Purity

It's no secret that men can easily become sexually stimulated simply by looking at a woman. Therefore it's important that you monitor the "eye gate." Though you may have no intentions whatsoever of committing adultery with the body, you might just be committing adultery with your eyes. Jesus spoke about that when He said, "Whoever looks at a woman to lust for her has already committed adultery with her in his heart" (Matthew 5:28).

A key part of marital intimacy is purity. Your wife is to keep herself pure for you, and God asks you to do the same for her. In your case, that purity starts with your eyes. Make a covenant with God and let Him know you desire to monitor your eyes in a way that honors Him and your wife.

*God, may I glorify You in all I do, including what I look at and think about. Help me to see my eyes as windows to my heart, and strengthen me to let only pure light in. Amen.*

# Guarding
# the Gift

So much of what we see in our world today has sex connected to it. "Sex sells" is Madison Avenue's motto, and certain visual images on TV and on the magazines at checkout stands make it all the harder for a Christian man to keep his thoughts pure.

There is only one woman you are to enjoy in a sexual sense, and that is your wife. And if you remain faithful to her, you will know blessing and joy, according to these words from the book of Proverbs: "Drink water from your own cistern, and running water from your own well...Let your fountain be blessed, and rejoice with the wife of your youth... let her breasts satisfy you at all times; and always be enraptured with her love" (5:15,18-19).

> *Lord, the world has distorted Your tremendous gift of sex. Help my wife and me to enjoy the real thing by guarding our eyes and hearts and preserving the precious gift You have given us. Amen.*

# Keeping
the Peace

One very big hindrance to marital intimacy is anger. That's a key reason the Bible says, "Do not let the sun go down on your wrath" (Ephesians 4:26). In other words, don't go to bed angry.

Disagreements and spats usually fester and grow foul if they are allowed to continue unresolved. That's why you want to deal with them right away. A right relationship with your wife is more important than winning an argument. So restore that bond with your beloved with a willingness to say, "I'm sorry." When you pursue forgiveness and reconciliation, intimacy will naturally follow. So when conflict occurs, be sure to make up with each other quickly!

*Lord, when I'm angry, prompt me by Your Spirit to express my feelings in a controlled and loving way. And when my wife is angry, help me to not take her feelings too personally. Amen.*

# Money Matters

If you were to ask most marriage counselors to identify one of the top, if not *the* top, causes of conflicts in a marriage, I believe the majority would say it's money—how it is acquired, how it is spent, and by whom. That's why as husbands we need to make sure we are giving strong leadership in our marriage in the area of money management.

This means you need to exercise self-control when it comes to handling money yourself. In fact, the way your children handle money will depend on the example you set, and whether you take time to teach them how to use it wisely. Your efforts may save you and your children much heartache later on. How would you rate the example you are setting, and in what ways can you improve?

> *Lord, help me to embrace this responsibility—to give, save, and spend wisely and to train my children to do the same. May money management be a strength and not a weakness in our family. Amen.*

# God
# and Money

If others were allowed a peek at your checkbook, what would they see? Checks written to missionaries, to your church, to charities? And checks toward the necessities of life, the needs of your family, your children's education? Or would they see a long log of checks written for indulgences, excesses, frivolities, and fun?

While your checkbook may be a private matter with regard to the people around you, that's not the case with God. He knows your every expenditure; He knows your heart attitude toward money. What do you think God would say about the way you handle your finances? This doesn't mean you can't have fun occasionally. But a man after God's own heart will make sure that true needs and priorities are taken care of first.

> *God, I want my priorities to match Yours. May my expenditures demonstrate that I trust You and that I care about the things You care about. Thank You for leading and guiding me. Amen.*

# On Loan
# from God

The money and the things you own—who does it all belong to? Do you view your family, your possessions, and everything else as gifts from God that are on loan to you? The psalmist wrote, "The earth is the LORD's, and all its fullness, the world and those who dwell therein" (24:1).

So what then is your role? If God is the owner and you are the user, then you are a *steward* of God's gifts to you. And 1 Corinthians 4:2 says, "It is required in stewards that one be found faithful." How would you rate your stewardship of your family, your talents, your spiritual gifts, your body, your money? God rewards those who are faithful—so every effort you make toward good stewardship is well worthwhile.

*Lord, everything in the world is Yours—including the things You have entrusted to me. Make me a good and faithful steward, I pray, pleasing You in every financial transaction I make. Amen.*

# From Want to Contentment

Contentment—or the lack of it—can have a major impact on how you manage your money. Advertisers say, "You need this new car," or "You deserve a luxury vacation." And if you're not content with what you have, it becomes all too easy to go into debt in order to get that car or go on that vacation.

Our sinful flesh fights against contentment and is prone to the "wants" of life. It's when we learn contentment that we are able to hold on to money longer and spend more wisely. And the more careful you are, the more your children will see the fallacy of society's delusion that wealth and possessions bring happiness. Contentment, then, is a significant key to good money management, and to the spiritual health and well-being of your family.

> God, You have given me every reason to be content—and more! When my heart is restless, help me rest in You and enjoy the deep contentment of knowing that I am in Your care. Amen.

# Giving as
# God Leads

There are many opinions about how much we should give to the Lord. What makes this hard is that every person has different financial circumstances and needs. Fortunately we find a helpful example in the lives of the Christians in Macedonia (in what is now part of modern-day Greece). They were poor and afflicted, yet they were rich in love and obedience. They gave selflessly and generously to God for the needs of others (2 Corinthians 8:1-6).

These Christians gave "according to their ability" (verse 3). That's a good rule of thumb to follow—we ought to give at least "according to" how we have prospered (1 Corinthians 16:2). Don't let others set the standard for you. Ask God to place on your heart a sense for how much you can give cheerfully, selflessly, and generously.

*God, please help me stop comparing myself with others. Lead me as I consider how You would have me use the resources You have entrusted to me. I trust You to provide for me. Amen.*

# Real Satisfaction

When it comes to our finances, we need to follow Paul's example. He was able to say, "I have learned the secret of being content in any and every situation" (Philippians 4:12 NIV). Try learning how to say no to yourself in the "things" department. Try being content with what you have. Try being happy about what other people have. Try being content with "food and clothing" (1 Timothy 6:8). Try being content with "godliness" (verse 6).

When you are content, you will know real satisfaction—not only in the financial department, but the spiritual department as well!

*Father, You have given me all I need for life and godliness, and You have added more blessings than I can count. I am content when I consider all that You have done. Thank You. Amen.*

# Passing Through

We as Christians are in the world but we are not to be consumed with the things of this world (1 John 2:15). We are merely pilgrims who are passing through (1 Peter 2:11). We are citizens of heaven (Philippians 3:20), and we are to eagerly await the return of our King to reign here on the earth.

One sure solution to worldliness is to follow Paul's admonition to "set your mind on things above, not on things on the earth" (Colossians 3:2). When you focus on God, His Word, and spiritual priorities, you're less likely to succumb to the lures of the world. So "seek first the kingdom of God and His righteousness," and He will take care of the rest—"all these things shall be added to you" (Matthew 6:33).

*Lord, focusing on worldly things makes me anxious and discontented. But when I think about You and the tremendous work You are doing in and through me, I'm filled with confidence. Thank You!*

# Seeking
# God's Input

Since the money you manage really belongs to God, shouldn't you consult Him as to how you spend it? Hopefully you and your wife have already committed your budget to the Lord. Pray about your finances, and pray whenever it comes time to make a major purchase. Ask yourselves, "How will this purchase impact our budget?" And, "Is it wiser for us to repair the current car or appliance rather than buy a new one?"

As you prayerfully bring your financial decisions to God, you'll develop more and more of a steward's mind-set in all you do with your money. You're also less likely to make impulse spending decisions you'll regret later on. Prayer will help you slow down, make careful choices, and make the most of your resources.

*Lord, guide my wife and me as we endeavor to bring everything in our lives, including our finances, to You in prayer. Help us to apply what You're teaching us and to make wise decisions. Amen.*

# The Riches
# of Wisdom

The Bible repeatedly exhorts us to pursue wisdom. Simply defined, wisdom is the application of knowledge, and sometimes even plain old common sense.

How important is wisdom? Proverbs 24:3-4 says, "Through wisdom a house is built, and by understanding it is established. By knowledge the rooms are filled with all precious and pleasant riches."

Doesn't that make you want to grow in wisdom? The good news is God made it very accessible. In the Bible, we can find "all things that pertain to life and godliness" (2 Peter 1:3). So if you need wisdom as a man, husband, or father, turn to God's Word. In doing so, you'll build up your house and fill it "with all precious and pleasant riches."

*Lord, save me from foolishness and help me to grow in wisdom. Please transform my mind as I read Your Word, converse with people who know You, and seek You in prayer. Amen.*

# Praising God
# for His Gifts

When was the last time you thanked the Lord for the blessing of your home and the people in it? Don't ever take His gifts to you for granted. Love your home, care for it, and praise God for it. When it comes to thanking Him for what you have at home, you'll find a great example in King David, who said, "Who am I, O Lord GOD? And what is my house, that You have brought me this far?…You are great, O Lord GOD" (2 Samuel 7:18,22).

Does David's prayer and attitude reflect your heart? Can you humbly say, "Who am I, O Lord GOD? And what is my house, that You have brought me this far?" God has blessed you and your house; make a habit of thanking Him for all He has given you.

*God, save me from ever taking my family or our home for granted. Even in our hardest times, You have blessed us with so much more than we deserve. Thank You! Amen.*

# Passing on
# Your Faith

As a dad, have you ever considered that you can not impart to your kids what you do not possess yourself? Notice a parent's first responsibility, according to Moses: "You shall love the LORD your God with all your heart, with all your soul, and with all your strength. And these words which I command...you shall teach them diligently to your children" (Deuteronomy 6:5-7). Moses told parents to *first* love God themselves. Only then could they pass their faith on to their children.

Make it your chief aim in life to develop a living and growing love for God. Your children will notice this, and they will respond positively as they see what's important to you.

> *God, the last thing I want is to be a fake—someone who doesn't walk the talk. Whenever I'm teaching my kids, help me to look to my own life and make any necessary adjustments. Amen.*

# Your Greatest Investment

Time is always in such short supply for us men! We never seem to have enough of it. We are usually busy every spare minute. And sometimes it's a challenge to make sure our children get some of that time.

When it comes to the priority of time with children, I often tell men this paraphrased quote from Jesus: "What is a man profited if he gains the whole world, and loses or forfeits [his children]?" (Luke 9:25 NASB). Your kids are worth more than all the material wealth in the world. So it's vital to set aside time for them. Every moment you spend with them accumulates to become your greatest investment and will reap wonderful dividends.

> *God, help me to create great memories with my kids—memories of fun times with a dad who would do anything in the world for them because he loves them and loves You. Amen.*

# Setting Things Right

Y ou may have had times when you've felt utterly inadequate as a father. You've made a mess of things, and you've had your priorities in the wrong places. You haven't been the best example to your kids, and you might even feel like giving up on this parenting thing.

Well, if you're reading this book, that's a sign you want to do what is correct, so you're taking steps in the right direction. Your desire is to be a man after God's own heart, and that's what counts most. So ask God to forgive your past mistakes and to give you renewed energy for fulfilling your role as a father. As you yield yourself to God, He will carry on His work through you—and that will bring blessings upon your family.

> *Lord, my kids need a better dad. Make me that dad, I pray. Forgive me, free me from anything that would hold me back, and help me follow You, the best Dad of all. Amen.*

# Do They Know You Care?

It's funny what children will remember from their childhood. When you quiz them about the past, they might not recall the things you thought were so special, such as birthdays or certain gifts you gave to them. Rather, they're more likely to remember the special traditions you established in your family, such as your annual backpacking trip with the boys, or those monthly "date nights" with your girls.

When you develop such traditions, you show your children you care about them and want to spend time with them. That, in turn, creates an environment in which they feel comfortable sharing their hearts with you. The result? You grow closer together as family. All you have to do is give them your time…and, of course, a listening ear.

> Lord, help me to "be there" for my kids, to establish traditions that help them feel safe and loved. And help me make the most of every opportunity to show them I care. Amen.

# Honor
# Through Humility

Moses was one of the greatest leaders in all the Bible, and yet he is also an excellent example of humility. He worked for Jethro, his father-in-law, as a shepherd for 40 years. Then God met Moses at the burning bush and called him back to Egypt (Exodus 3:1-10). When Moses approached his father-in-law about leaving his job, he did so with humility: "Please let me go and return to my brethren who are in Egypt" (Exodus 4:18). Even though Moses had a divine call from God and was 80 years old, he didn't *tell* Jethro of his intentions to leave. Rather, he *asked* permission. This is what it means to honor your parents and in-laws—to treat them with humility. Sometimes that's hard to do, but with God's grace, it is possible.

*Lord, even though I don't live under my parents' roof, help me to show them the respect they deserve. Guard my tongue, I pray, and help me to speak only words that build them up. Amen.*

# Showing
# You Care

How are you doing at fulfilling the fifth commandment, which charges you to "honor your father and your mother" (Exodus 20:12)? This command isn't merely a suggestion; it's a mandate straight from God. How can you show honor to your parents and in-laws?

One way is to show real interest in what's going on in their lives. Do you personally call or write? Do you think about and pray for them? When you take time to communicate, you show that you care. And by staying in touch, you'll know how you can pray on their behalf.

Perhaps you don't live near your parents and in-laws. While distance may separate you, communication will unite you. So make an effort to show honor by reaching out, and you'll experience God's promised blessings.

*God, do my parents know that I really do care about them? Have I demonstrated my love for them? Show me the way as I resolve to give them the honor they deserve. Amen.*

# Extending Love
# Even When It's Hard

It's sad that many family relationships are not what God desires them to be. Relatives do things that hurt one another, causing anger, distrust, or separation. Don't be one who contributes to that! While you cannot change other people's hearts toward you, you can surely change yours toward them. "If it is possible, as much as depends on you, live peaceably with all men" (Romans 12:18).

So no matter what hinders family relationships, you can be the mature one who chooses to reach out and have a heart of forgiveness. And you can draw upon the resources of prayer, the Bible, and the power of the fruit of the Holy Spirit (Galatians 5:22-23) as you do so. By God's grace, you can extend love to your family.

*Lord, thank You for empowering me to forgive (or ask for forgiveness), to encourage, and to love. You can break down the walls between my family members, and I trust You to do just that. Amen.*

# God's Will
# in the Workplace

Over the years, men have often asked me how they could "know" God's will for their career. They thought if they had the answer, they would get a much clearer perspective on their jobs and their direction in life.

I tell them God's will regarding their work isn't some mystical revelation they have to hunt for. Rather, it's spelled out clearly in the Bible: "Whatever you do, do it heartily, as to the Lord and not to men" (Colossians 3:23), and "Be obedient to those who are your masters...not...as men-pleasers, but as bondservants of Christ" (Ephesians 6:5-6). When you see this as God's will for your job, it'll transform your attitude in the workplace—and have an incredibly positive impact on everyone around you!

> *God, it's great to know that by seeking You and retaining this mind-set, I can be confident that I'm in Your will. I choose to work heartily and honor my "masters"—because I honor You. Amen.*

# Letting God
# Use You

Many people are dissatisfied with their jobs, and they think the grass looks greener on the other side of the fence. What causes such discontent? One is a lack of purpose. They don't see their workplace as God's calling for their life. Another is a lack of understanding. They assume work will give their life meaning when it's actually service to God, family, and co-workers that does that. Yet another is disobedience. They see work as a means to pursue worldly success and possessions.

Commit to having a positive attitude at work and thanking God for where He has placed you. For when you are content, you'll work in harmony with God's plan for you—which will make you a much better worker.

*God, wherever I work, You lead me, You give my life meaning, and You provide everything I need. In You, I have it all—right where I am. Help me to glorify You at work today. Amen.*

# A Right Balance

Probably the greatest battle for every working man is striking the right balance between work and family life. God wants a husband and father to provide for his family and do his best on the job. But at the same time, God does not want him to work so much he neglects his family.

This calls for balance. Have you asked God to give you wisdom about this? Can you truly say you are giving your employer a fair day's work for a fair day's pay? And can you honestly evaluate whether your job is causing you to sacrifice on family relationships? What would other people say, including your wife and children? Have the courage to make necessary changes. When you make the right choices, God will bless you.

*Lord, thank You for my job and my family. They are gifts from You and important parts of Your calling on my life. Show me how to give myself to both in a balanced way. Amen.*

# Excelling for
# the Lord's Sake

When you do your job well, you bring glory to God. So hard work is a good thing. But today's culture has different ideas about work. Many people either want everything given to them without working for it, or they don't want to work very hard to get it. You, however, as a man after God's own heart, are different. You understand God's purposes and priorities for your life. You excel at work for God and His glory, and not for men. As a result, you'll reap blessings—from knowing you are doing God's will, from knowing your wife and family benefit from your provision, and from knowing you're giving your best in the task God has entrusted to you. These blessings and more will be yours when you tend to your career God's way.

*God, help me to be a worker who brings glory to You. When I am tired, may I have the satisfaction of knowing I've given my best and You will take care of the rest. Amen.*

# Making It Happen

Procrastination makes an unpleasant task even more painful. The longer you put it off, the more you'll have to deal with the negative consequences of not getting the job done.

Ask yourself: Why am I putting a project off? Does it seem too overwhelming? Then break it into smaller parts and do them one at a time. Are you delaying because you don't know where to begin? Swallow your pride and ask for advice. Whatever the holdup, find a way to begin moving forward. Get started...now! Once you've taken those first steps you'll gain momentum, and you'll find it easier to continue until you're finished. Then you'll know the good feeling of having that project behind you.

*God, am I stuck in a project at home or at work? Have I let others down by not following through? Show me where to invest my attention and how to move forward. Thank You. Amen.*

# Casting Your Burdens
## upon God

It's easy to let the cares of the world diminish the fun and joy you knew in the early years of marriage. These cares might include the press of limited finances, the pull of both of you working, the responsibilities of caring for children, the pressures of building a career, the problem of falling into a routine, or the predicament of poor health.

While you cannot ignore these cares, you can certainly yield them up to the Lord. Don't let life's pressures rob you of the joys of marriage. As 1 Peter 5:7 says, "Cast all your anxiety on him because he cares for you" (NIV). Letting God carry your burdens will free you to enjoy your marriage no matter what your circumstances.

*God, help me to trust You with the concerns on my heart today. May I know the joy of trusting You, and may that joy infect everyone in my household. Amen.*

# Serving Together

The most rewarding fun you can have in a marriage is serving the Lord together. That's because it has eternal value and blesses others along the way.

This can take shape in many forms. You can teach a class together. You can go to Christian camps and serve as volunteer workers. You can do behind-the-scenes jobs at church, such as setting up for class, getting refreshments ready, helping clean up after an activity, joining a prayer group, visiting the hospital or shut-ins, or writing letters and preparing care packages for missionaries or Third-World children.

This will definitely make a difference in your marriage—there's something about serving God as a couple that keeps you focused on Him and draws you closer together.

*Lord, forgive me for focusing so much on my own little world. Open my eyes to see the needs around me and the gifts You have given my wife and me to meet those needs. Amen.*

# Focusing on
# Your Family

When it comes to making time for your wife and kids, how about turning off the television for a night?

Before televisions were invented, families spent their evenings talking, planning trips and holidays, reading, and playing games together. The television has snatched all that away and substituted the warmth of personal involvement and fun with impersonal entertainment.

Set aside one night a week and use it to have fun with each other as a couple or with your family— without the distraction of television. The adjustment might be a bit hard at first, but in time, these evenings will become a cherished family tradition.

*God, an evening with no TV would be great, but taking that first step can be tough. I ask for wisdom and creativity so I can facilitate enjoyable interactions with my family. Amen.*

# Saved to Serve

Bud Wilkinson, the legendary coach of the University of Oklahoma football team from 1947 to 1963, once described the game of football as "50,000 people who desperately need exercise watching 22 men who desperately need rest." Unfortunately that is the situation in most churches today. Spiritually gifted believers are sitting in the pews watching a small handful of others do all the serving.

As Christians, we are saved to serve. Ephesians 2:10 says, "We are [the Lord's] workmanship, created in Christ Jesus for good works." A believer who isn't serving is like a car that's been put on blocks. That makes the car useless! Are you serving? God brought you into the church for the purpose of rendering useful and beneficial service.

*God, I don't want to be in the bleachers when You are calling me to be on the field. Help me find my position on Your team and fill it with the strength You provide. Amen.*

# A Living Sacrifice

Service that counts is service that costs. Think about it: We usually place less value on things that are given to us than on things we have paid for. The only difference in the Christian life is that our salvation didn't cost us anything. Rather, it cost God everything. He sent His only Son to the cross to pay the very high price for redeeming us from sin.

Shouldn't that make you and me willing to sacrifice ourselves for the sake of Christ's body, the church? He gave His life for us...and we ought to give our lives for Him in return. Paul put it this way: "Present your bodies a living sacrifice, holy, acceptable to God, which is your *reasonable service*" (Romans 12:1).

*Lord, I pray for a new perspective today. When I sacrifice my time or money or energy, help me to see how small those sacrifices really are compared to Your great sacrifice for the world. Amen.*

# Steps to Serving

If you are already actively serving God and His people, that's great. Keep it up! But if not, the question you should ask is, "How can I begin to serve?"

First, *be informed*. Read your Bible to get a better understanding of what spiritual gifts are and how they work. Start by reading 1 Corinthians 12 and Romans 12:3-8. Find out all you can about these "abilities." Second, *be willing*. This is the hardest part about getting started. God is not going to force you to serve Him. No, doing that is your choice. So what will you do? That brings up the last step—*be available*. Find an opportunity and sign up. And as you serve, you'll bring honor to God and blessings to others.

*God, please lead me as I step out into a new area of service. And help me capitalize on small opportunities to humbly serve people all around me in my everyday life. Amen.*

# Faithful in the
# Small Things

My service in the church began with washing pots and pans at socials and showing up for "workdays" on Saturday morning, during which we would do maintenance work around the property. As I grew spiritually, I was given other responsibilities. And as I was faithful, God moved me into greater areas of service. It all started with a willingness to serve, and God did the rest.

And the most exciting part? My wife, Elizabeth, got involved as well. As we both served, we grew spiritually—which brought greater blessings and fulfillment to our marriage. Yes, service will require personal sacrifice on your part. But the spiritual dividends you'll reap are well worthwhile.

*Lord, thank You for opportunities to say no to pride and yes to humble service. Throughout each day, please remind me that faithful service in the small things will lead to greater responsibilities. Amen.*

# Little Things, Big Difference

What's great about serving God is that there are many "little things" you can do to help other believers or the church, even if you don't have any training. It may seem a little thing to sweep the floors, pick up after the Sunday service, help with repairs around the building, set up chairs. But those little things are what make the big things go smoothly and contribute to making church a better experience for all. It's remarkable how that which may seem insignificant really does make a big difference.

So don't ever disdain the little things. Every bit of help counts. Every person has an important role. Maybe your work takes place behind the scenes, but God is paying attention. And He will reward you when you are faithful in the little things.

> *God, is my system of measurement different from Yours? Is a little act of service actually a big deal to You? Help me to see deeper meaning and greater value in "small" acts of service. Amen.*

# The Power of
# Your Actions

What if you don't feel comfortable about sharing your faith with your neighbors? Well, there are many ways you can build bridges with them so that your "comfort level" is no longer an issue.

For example, you can participate in neighborhood yard sales or block parties. Volunteer to feed your neighbors' pets while they are on vacation. Pick up their mail and bring in their newspapers. Water their garden or lawn. None of these activities require you to say a word about your beliefs. But your joyful spirit and servant attitude will speak volumes about your faith. Hopefully, as you give and expect nothing in return, your neighbors will want to know what makes you different. And that, in turn, will let you share with them. Who knows what God will do in their hearts?

*God, help my family to pay attention to others, to serve them, to pray for them, and to shine Your light in our neighborhood. Amen.*

# Who Can
# You Invite?

Your local church is God's gift to you and your family, and it is also God's gift to a lost world. Just as your family is blessed by the programs offered at your church, your neighbors and workmates can receive a blessing from them as well.

Don't be shy—be excited about what's going on there. Share that enthusiasm with others. They need the saving hand of Jesus, and your church is just the place where they might meet Him. Invite the neighborhood children to youth activities. Invite their parents to seminars on parenting and marriage. Take them with you to a family or couples' retreat. You do the praying and inviting, and let God take it from there.

*Lord, thank You for my church. It's not perfect, but You have called us together to fellowship, worship, learn, pray, and serve. Who can I invite to church today? Amen.*

# Compassion
# on Display

Some people think compassion is not a very "manly" emotion. But is that trait to be exhibited only by women? You know the answer, don't you? Jesus is the perfect example of a man who demonstrated this emotion. He sorrowed over people's unbelief (Luke 19:41). He wept for His friend Lazarus (John 11:35). When He saw people in need, "He was moved with compassion" (Matthew 9:36).

When was the last time you wept for the salvation of someone, or for a person who was deeply hurting? If compassion is not one of your strengths (and it should be, as you follow Christ's example), then pray and ask God to soften your heart so this quality is on display in your life.

> *Jesus, thank You for being an example of a compassionate man. I pray that my family, friends, and co-workers would all know that I care for them and that I'm moved by their concerns. Amen.*

# Letting God
# Do His Work

Every man hopes to have an impact on his world. But influence is costly, for it demands hard work. It takes time to build, and it involves helping other people. It is hard-won and easily lost. It takes responsibility, and it calls for sensitivity in your relationships with others. But that shouldn't discourage you. The good news is that, with God's help, influence is attainable by anyone.

When you look at the men in the Bible who had the greatest impact on others, you'll notice they all shared a key trait: They yielded their lives fully to God. They submitted their all to Him. As a result, God was free to work powerfully through them. And you can let God do the same through you.

*Lord, I choose to seek You and obey You today. As You work in my life, I trust that You will help me share simple words and acts of service so people are drawn to You. Amen.*

# Ordinary Person, Extraordinary God

The apostle Paul is a prime example of someone who had great influence. He spread the gospel far and wide, and wrote much of the New Testament. Have you noticed the qualities that set him apart are within your reach? He was obedient, he served others, he was humble, he prayed, he trusted God, he was empowered by the Spirit, he loved and read the Scriptures, and he was faithful in the tasks God gave him. In every way he was an ordinary person empowered by an extraordinary God.

You too can have great influence. It takes a willingness to do the basics God asks of every believer. And the best part is, you do it all in God's power. Isn't that amazing?

*God, as I seek You and humbly serve others today, may Your relationship with me grow deeper and Your influence through me grow broader. Thank You. Amen.*

# It's Never
# Too Late

Paul was an amazingly influential believer—and yet did you know he got a late start in the Christian life? Most people become Christians as teens and young adults; Paul didn't get started in formal ministry until he was past 40. Most pastoral search committees would never consider a man in his mid-forties with little to no experience! And remember—back in those days, someone that age was pretty old.

In spite of his late start, Paul had a great impact. This teaches us two important lessons: (1) It's never too late to start serving God, and (2) it's never too late to change the course of your life so you can make a difference. No matter what your age or circumstance, God can always use you.

*Lord, help me believe that You can influence other people for good through me. Today I turn away from my excuses for holding back, and I choose to serve the people You bring my way. Amen.*

# Staying
the Course

When hardships come, many Christians feel like checking out. When life goes wrong, when finances get worse, when a job becomes difficult, or family life falls apart, they say, "I've had it. I quit. I don't see God helping me. I'm just not cut out for the Christian life."

If that ever happens to you, remember this: God can work through adversity. And He is with you at all times when life gets rough. Consider Paul—he was persecuted, beaten, jailed, and threatened with death. But he didn't falter. He waited on God and trusted Him. And he said, "I can do all things through Christ who strengthens me" (Philippians 4:13). From Paul you learn that hardship can be the training ground for a life of impact.

> *God, I don't enjoy hardships. But if they come with the package of serving You, and if You can use them to make me a better man, then I'll stay the course and follow You. Amen.*

# All Things
# Are Possible

Maybe you've wondered if God can really use you. You don't have much training, you're getting a late start in life, or adversity has held you back a lot. Or maybe it's something as simple as the fact you're a relatively new believer and you don't know your Bible well yet.

If so, you're in good company. In the Bible we find many people who found themselves in similar predicaments—yet God worked mightily through them. This affirms an important truth: "With God all things are possible" (Matthew 19:26).

All that to say, don't ever let a supposed lack of qualifications or seemingly prohibitive circumstances get you down. God is able...and He will enable you.

*Lord, I'm not qualified to play much of a part in Your kingdom. But You do incredible things through underdogs, so today I'll focus less on my weakness and more on Your strength. Amen.*

# In Control
# of the Future

Life is full of surprises. You never know when things may take a sudden and unexpected turn for the worse. And when they do, you may find yourself saying, "What happened?"

You can take comfort in the fact God is never caught by surprise. He is in control of the future, and He will never allow you into a situation beyond your ability to handle. That doesn't mean He will make life easier for you—just that He will sustain you and enable you to persevere. As God said to Paul, "My grace is sufficient for you, for My strength is made perfect in weakness" (2 Corinthians 12:9). When you trust God in your weakness, His grace will hold you and shine forth.

*God, I don't know what's going to happen, but You know every potential outcome. I don't adapt or execute very well, but You can do anything. Thank You for pouring Your strength into me today. Amen.*

# A Great Treasure

The Bible is a truly remarkable book. And the more you know about it, the more you'll appreciate it. Consider what Psalm 19:7-11 says:

*It is the perfect law* (verse 7). The Bible has no errors. It is historically accurate and provides spiritual truth.

*It is a rule book for daily living* (verse 8). Scripture is always 100 percent right. You can trust what it says about how to live.

*It is eternal* (verse 9). Other books come and go, but the Bible endures forever.

*It is a treasure* (verse 10). It contains everything you need for life and godliness (2 Peter 1:3). Nothing else can do that.

> *Father, thank You for reminding me today that the Bible is an incredible treasure. Open my ears and eyes so I can receive Your truth and respond accordingly. Amen.*

# A Help at All Times

What are some ways the Bible helps you? Again, look at what Psalm 19:7-11 says:

*It refreshes and heals.* The Bible converts the sinner and restores the believer who stumbles (verse 7).

*It gladdens the heart.* Scripture is a source of true joy (verse 8).

*It illuminates the mind.* The Bible gives meaning to life (verse 8).

*It satisfies.* As food satisfies the body, Scripture satisfies the soul (verse 10).

*It rewards.* There is no greater reward than a clean conscience, a pure heart, and peace of mind. All this comes not just from *knowing* God's Word, but *keeping* it (verse 11).

> *Lord, I pray that every time the culture around me suggests a path to happiness, You will remind me that true and lasting satisfaction comes through knowing You in Your Word. Amen.*

# Soaking in
# the Word

To what extent are you allowing Scripture to do its empowering work in your life?

It's not enough to interact with the Bible on a superficial level. If you really want to know the power of God's Word, it needs to "dwell in you richly" (Colossians 3:16). That means reading it and studying it. As the apostle Paul told his disciple Timothy, "Be diligent to present yourself approved to God, a worker who does not need to be ashamed, rightly dividing the word of truth" (2 Timothy 2:15). When you let God's Word thoroughly permeate you, you'll receive the wisdom, maturity, and strength you need for living a victorious Christian life. In fact, your life will become something others want—and want to follow.

*God, I pray Your Word will go deep into the core of my being. Help me cooperate with Your work in my life by giving Scripture the time, priority, and respect it deserves. Amen.*

# Going Against
# the Grain

Living according to God's Word is a tall order in today's immoral society. For that matter, it's never been easy to live for God—not in Paul's day, not in the days since the sexual revolution, nor during any other period in Christian history.

Yet God wants you to be His man—a man who has resolve to live according to Scripture. A man who cares more about pleasing God than pleasing people.

And He has given you the resources to stand strong in the face of opposition. When you respond to God and allow His Word to fill you, the Holy Spirit will empower you with the courage you need to persevere and live in obedience rather than compromise.

*Lord, may this be a good day—a day of standing strong against disobedience and compromise, a day filled with Your Word and the power of the Holy Spirit. Amen.*

# Unlimited Potential

There's no way to adequately describe all the ways God's Word can change you. This list only scratches the surface: The Bible can equip you for every good work (2 Timothy 3:17), stimulate your spiritual growth (Acts 20:32), give you wisdom (Proverbs 4:11), give you peace (Proverbs 3:1-2), give you direction (Psalm 119:105), keep you from sin (Psalm 119:11), give you power (Colossians 1:11), and give you discernment for godly living (Hebrews 5:14).

Notice I didn't say, "The Bible *will*..." I said, "The Bible *can*..." All the power and potential you need for change and growth is available—when you look to God's Word, learn God's Word, and keep God's Word.

> *Father, thank You for giving me all I need to become more like You. Today I choose to do my part—to take in Your Word and follow it as You empower me. Amen.*

# The Blessing
# of Confession

Unconfessed sin always hinders your progress toward spiritual maturity. So to ensure that your growth remains steady and uninterrupted, keep a short record of sins with God. Confess any and all sins to Him right away. If you want to experience a close, ongoing relationship with Him, do as David did in Psalm 32 and admit your sins, whether big or small. There, David confessed his affair with Bathsheba and his subsequent murder of her husband (2 Samuel 11). Make confession a habit so you can experience the wonderful cleansing that comes afterward.

David wrote in Psalm 32:1, "Blessed is he whose transgression is forgiven, whose sin is covered." Don't try to hide your sin—lift it upward to God and ask for His forgiveness. Then you'll know blessing and growth.

*God, You know everything about me...and love me anyway! Thank You in advance for forgiving me and healing me as I talk with You about my failures. Amen.*

# Persevering
# in Prayer

Prayer is a spiritual discipline that is difficult for even the most devout Christian to practice on a truly consistent basis. It demands time and requires focus, which are hard for modern minds and lifestyles to accommodate. To pray in dependence upon God also requires us to overcome our natural tendency to try to come up with our own solutions to life's problems. Prayer tries our patience. We dislike waiting on God for His answers. So we try to manipulate our situation by coming up with our own quick answers.

Don't let the struggle to pray discourage you. Ask God to keep you from being distracted by the world around you, to give you a God-focus, and to help you wait patiently for His answers. That will help you to persevere in this vital area of your Christian life.

*Father, sometimes I feel like a child who is just learning to talk to his dad. Thank You for being even more excited about my faltering attempts than that dad is about his son's first words. Amen.*

# Praying
# with Confidence

When you pray to God, you are talking to someone you can't see, someone whose existence is tangibly validated only by what you see of His handiwork in creation (Romans 1:20) or by the revelation of Himself in the Bible. So prayer is the purest form of faith, which is described as "the substance of things hoped for, the evidence of things not seen" (Hebrews 11:1). Yet the faith of prayer is not based on vivid imagination or wishful thinking. It is based on the promises of God, which are found in the Bible.

Scripture says, "There has not failed one word of all His good promise" (1 Kings 8:56). God has a perfect track record when it comes to keeping His promises. Therefore you can pray with confidence that God will fulfill every single one.

> *God, talking with someone I can't see isn't always easy. But I can see what You have revealed about Yourself in the Bible, and that's enough for me to have confidence in You. Amen.*

# Waiting for God's Answers

When you think your prayers aren't being answered, you tend to get discouraged and cry out, "God, why aren't You helping me?"

Yet God has promised to answer your prayers: "Ask, and it will be given to you; seek, and you will find; knock, and it will be opened to you" (Matthew 7:7). However, sometimes you don't see the answer for a while, or God may say no because He has a different—and better—plan.

So you are exhorted to ask. But your request must be...

- in faith (Matthew 21:22),

- without selfish motives (James 4:3), and

- according to the will of God (1 John 5:14-15).

*Lord, I confess that I'm not good at waiting for Your answers to my prayers. But as I wait, I believe You will build my faith, purify my heart, and show me Your will. Thank You!*

# Too Busy
# to Pray?

Often when you fail to pray, you say it's because you're so busy. But in reality, it's not your schedule that keeps you from praying. It's your failure to realize the importance of prayer and *make* the time to pray.

And instead of relying upon the power of prayer in all that you do, you turn to your feeble wisdom and energy. You roll up your sleeves and get busy, turning to your own power instead of God's.

If your life is so busy you can't pray, have you ever considered it's because you haven't taken time to ask God for help with your priorities? Turn to Him, and He will give you the discernment that enables you to use your time well so that you are able to pray.

*God, show me—what have I prioritized above my time with You? What have I depended on instead of You? Help me assess my priorities today and keep prayer at the top of the list. Amen.*

# When You
# Need Wisdom

Are you experiencing a difficult problem in your life right now? Are you at a crossroad with regard to a major decision? Are you struggling with issues you don't have answers for? If yes, hear this promise from your heavenly Father: "If any of you lacks wisdom, let him ask of God, who gives to all liberally and without reproach, and it will be given to him" (James 1:5).

God stands ready to give you wisdom. Remember, He is the source of it: "Oh, the depth of the riches both of the wisdom and knowledge of God!" (Romans 11:33). And when you don't understand what is happening, you need to wait, trust Him, and rest in His care. He is always faithful to His own.

*Lord, I'll be the first to admit it—I need Your wisdom! Help me to wait on You and to put into practice the things You show me in Your Word. Amen.*

# Saying Yes to God

God is able to use a man who is willing to do whatever He says. By this I mean a person who listens to and obeys Him.

We see confirmation of this in the Bible. For example, the apostle Paul was asked to *get up*—and spread the gospel. Abraham was asked to *give up*—to sacrifice his son Isaac up to God, until God spared Isaac. Moses was asked to *speak up*—to confront Pharaoh about letting the people of Israel go. And Daniel was asked to *stand up*—to not yield to demands to compromise his faith. In every case, God rewarded the obedience these men showed.

When you yield yourself in complete and wholehearted obedience to God, He can do great things through you.

*Father, show me how I can honor You in everything I do at home, at work, and when I'm just having fun. I choose in advance to say yes to You in all I do! Amen.*

# The Power
# of Obedience

When you consider the extraordinary ways God worked through men such as Moses and Paul, you may think, *I can't measure up to people like them. I don't have what they had.*

But you must realize that these "heroes" of the faith were just common, ordinary people. It was their obedience—their complete yieldedness to God—that gave them uncommon strength and faith. They submitted their lives to God, which freed God to work through them.

I don't know about you, but their examples inspire me to re-evaluate my own obedience. Am I reluctant to listen to God because I think He is asking the impossible? Am I failing to make myself available to Him because I'm doubtful or afraid? Your part is to simply obey, and God will do His part.

*God, I see now that You can do anything through me if I will simply yield myself to You. Help me to make myself more available to You today. Amen.*

# At the Center
## of God's Will

Do you know what I believe is the icing on the cake of obedience, what I believe to be one of the most compelling reasons for choosing to obey God? It is this: Obedience leads to a powerful, confident life. When you are obedient, and when you allow yourself to be led by God through the unexpected, you then have a confidence based on the fact that you know you are exactly where God wants you to be. You won't find yourself doubting the circumstances in your life or the direction things are going. You'll have the inner peace and joy that comes from knowing you are at the center of God's will!

*Lord, thank You for leading me to the center of Your will. Help me to see Your hand in everything that comes my way as I follow You today. Amen.*

# God-confidence

Are you fearful because God appears to be moving you in an unexpected direction? Is the unknown causing you to waver on the path of obedience? Take heart in your resolve. Walk in confidence with God. Walk as King David did, declaring, "Though I walk through the valley of the shadow of death, I will fear no evil; for You are with me" (Psalm 23:4).

Though you might not know where God's will is taking you, you can trust God to watch over and stay with you. Though life may take surprising turns, they are not unexpected to God. He knows what is happening and why, and all He calls you to do is to trust Him.

*Father, I affirm that as long as You lead me and I walk with You, I have nothing to fear. I resolve to follow You today, knowing that I'm never safer than when I'm with You. Amen.*

# Making the Best Decisions

What if you're uncertain about an important decision you must make? How can you seek God's input? Here are the four C's you'll find helpful for the times when you need guidance:

Commands from the inspired Word of God

Competent and wise counselors

Circumstances and changing conditions

Conscience aided by the Holy Spirit

God can use any or all of these means to give direction to you if you are ready to listen. It may take time, but that's okay. Making use of these resources will help you to make informed choices that honor and glorify God.

*God, I want to make wise decisions that glorify You. Help me to keep my eyes and ears open so I can learn from You and honor You in all I say and do. Amen.*

# Great Is
# His Faithfulness

How often do you take time to pause and revel in how faithful God has been to you?

Recognizing God's good help to you is important. It's when you remember His unceasing care that you are reminded He will carry you through every situation in life, no matter how bad. It was God's faithfulness in adversity that led King David to write, "I waited patiently for the LORD; and He inclined to me, and heard my cry. He also brought me up out of a horrible pit, out of the miry clay, and set my feet upon a rock, and established my steps. He has put a new song in my mouth—praise to our God; many will see it and fear, and will trust in the LORD" (Psalm 40:1-3).

*Lord, You've pulled me out of a few "horrible pits" and established my steps. Help me to never forget what You have done, to always praise You, and to eagerly share Your faithfulness with others. Amen.*

# When It's Hard
# to Have Hope

When something terrible happens in your life, are you ever tempted to ask, "What good could come out of this?" It *looks* like a disaster. It *feels* like a disaster. Therefore you conclude, "It *is* a disaster!"

That's when you want to remember God's promise, "I know the thoughts that I think toward you... thoughts of peace and not of evil, to give you a future and a hope" (Jeremiah 29:11). And then there's Romans 8:28, which says, "All things work together for good to those who love God."

God doesn't tell you you'll escape suffering or pain. Rather, He promises to miraculously use even bad situations for your ultimate good, and He assures you that you have a great future ahead of you. Let these promises sustain you when you find it's hard to have hope.

*Father, when I suffer, please strengthen me with Your Word and Your Spirit so I can endure with joy, knowing that You ultimately have great things in store for me. Amen.*

# Always There
# with You

Do you ever think about the fact that God knows, in advance, everything that will happen?

That means there is nothing that takes God by surprise—even the difficult crises in your life. So when you find yourself worried about tomorrow, lift your cares up to the Lord. He has already seen the future, and because He is faithful, He will give you whatever you need to persevere through your problems. In the same way that He sustained the psalmist "through the valley of the shadow of death" (Psalm 23:4), He will preserve and comfort you in every trial you face. That's why you can rejoice with David and say, "Surely goodness and mercy shall follow me all the days of my life" (verse 6).

*God, I don't know what might happen tomorrow, but You do. I can't cause good to come from any crisis, but You can. I won't always be able to meet my own needs, but You will. Thank You.*

# Letting
# God Lead

When you submit yourself to God and obey Him, you allow Him to do what He desires in your life. You make it possible for Him to lead you wherever He wants to use you.

At the same time, you'll experience the confidence that comes from knowing you are exactly where God wants you to be. You'll experience the joy of knowing you are at the center of God's will. Then you, along with Paul, can confidently lead and boldly influence others as you declare, "Imitate me, just as I also imitate Christ" (1 Corinthians 11:1).

That's why obeying God is so important. It allows Him to work through you, and it gives you a secure confidence for everyday living. Isn't that what you long for?

*God, when I'm intimidated by a huge task before me, help me to focus on simply obeying You one step at a time. And may my life encourage others to do the same. Amen.*

# Attending to His Word

If you struggle with obeying God, ask Him to give you the strength to obey His commands. And that strength will come as you...

- faithfully read His Word,
- faithfully hear the preaching of His Word,
- faithfully listen to wise counsel from His Word, and
- faithfully deal with sin in your life as revealed by the piercing light of His Word.

Can you see how God's Word is such an important part of your life? Your willingness to obey the Lord is a key step toward experiencing God's blessings, and it will enable you to become a man God can use to make a difference.

*Lord, thank You for pouring Your strength into me as I attend to Your Word. May every blessing and every trial in my life turn my obedient attention to Your Word. Amen.*

# Keeping Your Eye
## on the Prize

Because obedience has its challenges, it's the less-traveled path. Disobedience, on the other hand, is the more well-worn way. In fact, it is characterized by gridlock! Why? Because it's the easy way out. It's the road we're tempted to take when things get sticky or uncomfortable. It's the path of least resistance, and sadly, it's the path that makes us men of little or no positive impact.

As you run the race for Christ, you'll face hurdles that trip you up, knock you down, or pressure you to compromise God's standards. That's why Paul urges you to "press toward the goal for the prize of the upward call of God in Christ Jesus" (Philippians 3:14). If you keep your eye on the prize at the finish line, you'll have what it takes to overcome life's challenges.

*God, instead of sneaking around the hurdles of life on the path of least resistance, I want to sail over those challenges on the high road of obedience. Please help me. Amen.*

# All Ear

Have you ever tried to define *obedience*? That's the challenge a missionary ran up against as he was translating the Bible into a foreign language. Taking a break from his search for a meaning, he called to his dog. When the dog came running, a tribal observer said, "Your dog was all ear." Instantly the missionary had the words he needed to define *obedience*—"to be all ear."

How about you? Are you "all ear" when it comes to hearing what God says in His Word?

Ask the Lord to help you respond with eagerness to Scripture. You'll find this easier to do when you follow the example set by King David: "Your word I have hidden in my heart, that I might not sin against You" (Psalm 119:11).

> *Father, as I hide Your Word in my heart, help me to listen to its promptings and hear its life-giving message. And then, give me strength to obey—to be all ear. Amen.*

# Enduring Opposition

Anytime you stand up for what you believe, you will experience opposition—you can count on it! As Paul told his young disciple, Timothy, *"All* who desire to live godly in Christ Jesus will suffer persecution" (2 Timothy 3:12).

Earlier in 2 Timothy, Paul wrote, "You...must endure hardship as a good soldier of Jesus Christ. No one engaged in warfare entangles himself with the affairs of this life" (2:3-4). You are called to live boldly by different standards—God's standards.

Yes, it will be difficult. But such hardship is nothing compared to what you'll gain—God's blessing for your obedience and a clear conscience for doing what is right.

> *God, how are You asking me to stand up for what I believe today? When opposition comes my way, give me strength to bear it with grace and maintain a clear conscience. Amen.*

# Tapping into God's Strength

The beauty of obedience is that what God *expects* you to do, He also *enables* you to do. The strength comes from Him. You just need a willing heart.

The apostle Paul wrote, "Be strong in the Lord and in the power of His might" (Ephesians 6:10). God has made this strength available to you, and it's pretty remarkable. Paul spoke of "the *exceeding greatness* of His power toward us who believe, according to the working of His mighty power" (Ephesians 1:19).

The power of God triumphs over all else. And you have access to it. How? Through full dependence upon Him, "praying always with all prayer and supplication in the Spirit" (6:18).

*Lord, this is amazing. When I say yes to You—and mean it—You will give me the strength to follow through. Thank You for the "exceeding greatness" of Your power in me! Amen.*

# The Key
# to Focus

Have you ever felt like your life is scattered, as if you're going ten different directions? Have you wished your life was more focused?

If there's one lesson we can learn from the apostle Paul, it's the value of discipline. All his energies were passionately channeled in one direction—toward winning a "crown that will last forever" (1 Corinthians 9:25 NIV). Whereas many people chase after earthly prizes, or crowns that won't last, Paul pursued an eternal prize. He wanted to know Christ, the power of His resurrection, and the fellowship of His sufferings (Philippians 3:10). And he counted everything else but loss (3:3-7).

What is motivating you? Is Christ truly first in your life? When He is, you'll have focus.

*God, I want to be passionate, focused, and directed. Alert me today if I start going several directions at once. Bring all my responsibilities together into a unified life of following You. Amen.*

# The Rewards
of Discipline

I'm sure you've heard the slogan "No pain, no gain." Usually we see those words posted in a gym or over a locker-room door. But these same four words are also a perfect paraphrase of the personal philosophy of the apostle Paul, who said, "I strike a blow to my body and make it my slave so that...I myself will not be disqualified for the prize" (1 Corinthians 9:27 NIV).

This kind of discipline requires effort and sacrifice. But it's well worthwhile, for you'll receive a double prize—the eternal prize Paul is talking about, and the earthly prize of accomplishment and impact. Indeed, personal discipline brings great rewards.

*Father, as I focus on the prize right now, the effort, sacrifice, and pain of discipline seem much more manageable. Help me to focus on the prize all through the day today. Amen.*

# Mastering
# God's Word

When I was young in the Christian faith, a man came to our church to teach a seminar. It was evident that he knew his Bible very well. I admired his grasp of Scripture, and wished I had the same.

After the seminar, I summoned the courage to ask how he came to know the Bible so well. I expected him to say it was his theological training, or his ability to interpret Scripture. But to my surprise, he said it was a lifetime of just reading the Bible regularly, day in and day out.

That's pretty simple, isn't it? What a joy it was to realize every believer could have the same kind of knowledge. All it takes is faithful and consistent reading.

*Lord, I pray that You would open my eyes as I read the Scriptures. May my heart be like good soil so the seed of Your Word will go deep and produce a good crop. Amen.*

# The Value
of Goals

What are your goals in life? Have you defined them yet? Goals can help you in a lot of ways. For example, goals give *definition*—they take daydreams and make them concrete. Goals give *focus*—they help you know how to spend your time, and set aside time-wasters. Goals give *motivation*—they give you something to aim for, they help prod you onward when the going gets rough. Goals help you with *decision-making*—they equip you to make the best decisions about how to spend your time, money, and energy. And goals help you to have an *impact*—when you achieve them, you'll have grown as a person and hopefully others will benefit from your efforts.

So set some goals...and become the kind of man who makes a difference!

> *Lord, guide me as I assess my goals today. Help me set constructive goals, prioritize them appropriately, and submit them to Your leadership. May my goals lead to my highest goal of knowing You. Amen.*

# Using Time Well

The sooner we realize that life is but a vapor (James 4:14), the more likely we are to make sure we are using our time well.

That doesn't mean you can't take time to have fun and relax. Rather, it means making sure you have your priorities in order. At the top of the list is your spiritual health. That's because it affects everything else you do. When things are right between you and God and you're spending time in His Word, that will help you align the rest of your priorities properly, which include caring for your family, managing your finances wisely, maintaining good physical health, giving your best on the job, and serving others in your church. When you've taken care of these priorities, you can be confident you are using your time well.

*Father, do my priorities bring glory to You? Do they help me make the most of my short time on this earth? Help me re-evaluate my priorities and make any necessary adjustments. Amen.*

# The Gift
of Friends

Friends are a gift from the Lord. You should cultivate friendships with other men, especially other
Christian men who will encourage you in your faith
and give good advice. The Bible says, "As iron sharpens iron, so a man sharpens the countenance of his
friend" (Proverbs 27:17).

Are you friends with men who are a positive influence on your life, who encourage and build you up
in the faith? And are you making the effort to grow
spiritually so you, in turn, can be that kind of friend
to others?

If you are in need of such friends, ask God to lead
you to the right people. And be willing to take time
to be a friend to other men who would benefit from
your wisdom and experience.

> *Lord, help me to build replenishing friendships
> with other men. Whom can I look to as an exam-
> ple? Whom can I encourage? Thank You for my
> friends! Amen.*

# Understanding Temptation

When it comes to *temptation* and *sin*, there's an important distinction to make: Temptation is not sin. When you are tempted, you are faced with a choice. You still have the opportunity to resist and not fall into sin. But when you succumb, then you've gone from temptation to sin.

So if you find yourself struggling with temptation, you haven't done anything wrong yet. Just make sure you look to God for help, for He has promised, "No temptation has overtaken you except such as is common to man; but God is faithful, who will not allow you to be tempted beyond what you are able, but with the temptation will also make the way of escape, that you may be able to bear it" (1 Corinthians 10:13).

> *Lord, thank You for the promise that You will help me to bear every temptation that comes my way today. When I am tempted, help me remember to run to You. Amen.*

# Winning
# the Battle

When it comes to temptation, you are not alone. The Bible says this struggle is "common to man" (1 Corinthians 10:13). That means we all battle with temptation and sin. And thankfully, God has given you the resources you need for victory:

a new law (life in Christ),
a guide (the Holy Spirit),
a guidebook (the Bible),
and guides (wise counselors).

So you are fully equipped to withstand the temptations you face each day. Statements of "I can't" no longer apply to us. In Jesus Christ, it's "I can!" As Paul said, "I *can* do all things through Christ who strengthens me" (Philippians 4:13).

*God, I affirm that You have given me everything I need to win the battle over temptation. When I am tempted, please help me remember to say, "In Christ, I can defeat this!" Amen.*

# Leading
# by Serving

I'm sure you agree that Jesus Christ was the most influential man who ever lived. No one has or ever will match the impact He had.

What makes Him all the more remarkable is He wasn't an autocrat, a leader running roughshod over people or demanding respect and obedience. Rather, He was a humble servant. He "did not come to be served, but to serve, and to give His life" (Mark 10:45). After He performed the lowly task of washing the disciples' feet, He said, "I have given you an example, that you should do as I have done to you" (John 13:15).

Whose feet could you wash today? What opportunities do you have right now to serve rather than be served?

*Jesus, You are the King of kings and Lord of lords, yet You chose to live as a humble servant. May I follow in Your steps today as You give me opportunities to serve those around me. Amen.*

# For the
# Good of Others

By definition, serving others means being willing to make sacrifices for their good. A supreme example of this is the Good Samaritan in Luke 10:30-37. He sacrificed time by stopping to help the wounded traveler. He sacrificed his possessions by bandaging and dressing the man's wounds. He sacrificed his personal transportation by carrying the man to an inn. He sacrificed his life by taking care of the man personally. And he sacrificed his money by giving a day's wages and in essence a blank check to an innkeeper for the continued care of the wounded man.

Do you think the Good Samaritan had a positive impact? Without a doubt! When you serve, then, don't focus on what you've given up, but on what others have gained.

*God, all I have is Yours. Help me to joyfully sacrifice my time and possessions for others today, mindful that You will supply all I need according to Your riches in glory in Christ Jesus. Amen.*

Ps 1:9-10

I will praise You, O Lord, among the peoples
I will sing to You among the Nations

For Your Mercy reaches unto the
heavens and Your truth unto
the clouds

I want to live my life believing God. For much is at stake, and to much adventure stands to be missed. My faith pleases God and invites such uncomparable divine intervention in my life. I want to exercise it lavishly.

We have to receive faith from God to offer it back!

# When the Going Gets Tough

A servant of God is willing to endure pain, suffering, and persecution in order to accomplish God's work. Remember the apostle Paul? He faced tremendous adversity—prisons, beatings, and even shipwreck. Yet his ministry bore much fruit—all because he was willing to keep going.

How firm are you in your commitment to serve? Do you give up easily at the least sign of resistance? Or are you willing to withstand the opposition that often arises in the course of serving the Lord?

When you find yourself getting discouraged, remember the examples of Paul and Jesus. They paid a great price, yet realized even greater gains. Hang in there, for what you do will reap eternal rewards.

*God, thank You for strengthening me with all power according to Your glorious might so that I may have great endurance and patience. Because You are committed to me, I can be committed to You. Amen.*

# A Life
# Without Regrets

Paul saw his life as a sacrificial offering to God. He wrote, "I am already being poured out as a drink offering, and the time of my departure is at hand. I have fought the good fight, I have finished the race, I have kept the faith" (2 Timothy 4:6-7).

Because Paul had given his all, he could say he was ready to leave earth. He didn't have any regrets haunting him. With the Lord's help, he had done his job well, like a soldier who has completed his mission or a runner who has finished a race.

Are you living so that in the end you will have no regrets? Endeavor, by God's grace, to live each day to its fullest, and to give your all.

> *Lord, the race is long, but I am committed to run-*
> *ning well as You fill me with strength. Empower*
> *me to live this very day in such a way that I will*
> *finish it with no regrets. Amen.*

# Committing to Excellence

Legendary football coach Vince Lombardi said, "The quality of your life will be determined by the depth of your commitment to excellence, no matter what your chosen field." With that in mind, here are some questions you can ask yourself:

- What are the most important commitments in my life?
- Can I honestly say I'm giving my best to those commitments?
- How can I do better at carrying out those commitments, and what price am I willing to pay to make that happen?

Those questions will help you evaluate your priorities, and your answers will enable you to determine how to best spend your time and energy.

*Lord, help me to be honest today as I assess what I'm actually committed to. Do I need to reprioritize my commitments? What steps do I need to take to follow through? Lead me, Lord. Amen.*

# Going Beyond
# What Is Expected

To excel at something is to go over and above the normal. It means doing more than what is expected. It's about taking the extra step, the extra time, the extra effort in whatever you do. Yes, it's hard work, but in the end, if you persevere, it'll pay off.

Taking extra time with your wife and children will result in closer, stronger relationships with them. Going the extra mile on the job will gain appreciation from your boss and co-workers. Giving that extra effort as you serve in your church or help someone in need will bring blessing to others.

Without question, it pays to give your very best. Won't you ask the Lord to strengthen your resolve to strive for excellence in all that you do?

*Father, show me today where I have been cutting corners. Empower me through Your Word and Spirit to go beyond what is expected and to demonstrate Your amazing love. Amen.*

# A Pattern
# to Follow

Jesus was the greatest mentor of all time. He took a ragtag group of uneducated, ill-equipped men and, in three years, molded them into a force that turned the world upside down. Here's what we can learn from His example:

*There can be no impact without contact.* Jesus spent time with His men. He taught by word and example, cared for them, and was patient with them.

*He looked for men who were willing to learn.* When He called them to the ministry, they eagerly followed. They made mistakes, but were willing to listen and obey.

*He expected His disciples to make disciples.* Jesus commanded them to carry on His work. We're now a part of that work, and we're to pass it on to others.

> *Lord, empower me today to follow Your example. Help me to pay attention to others, to learn from them, and to offer my input when they are willing to receive it. Amen.*

# Your
# Legacy

What will you leave behind when you are gone? As you well know, only that which is spiritual will last. If all you leave behind are personal memories, they will fade with time. If you leave financial security and provisions, that will take care of people's temporary physical needs, but nothing more.

By contrast, if you leave a godly example and you've helped people grow more spiritually strong, you'll have given gifts that last for eternity. You'll have left treasures that can be passed on to future generations of believers. That, in a very real way, is what it means to "lay up for yourselves treasures in heaven" rather than on earth (Matthew 6:19-20).

*God, how is my heavenly treasure account doing? Show me today some simple ways that I can make a lasting impression on others and help them follow You. Amen.*

# Men
# Growing Men

You are most likely very grateful for those spiritually mature men who have taken the time to help you grow as a Christian. Likewise, everything you do for the next generation of Christian men will elicit their gratitude as well.

When it comes to choosing the right men to pour your life into, what should you look for?

- Look for *faithful* men. Find men who are trustworthy, who keep their word.
- Look for *available* men. Find men who are willing to sacrifice their time for ministry training.
- Look for *teachable* men. Find men who are eager to learn. Their hunger will ensure your time and energy are well-spent.

*Lord, the thought of pouring my life into younger Christians is a bit intimidating. Open the doors, I pray, and help me to simply share with others the things You have taught me. Amen.*

# A Living Bible

Have you ever considered that for some people in your life, you might be the only Christian they know? They may see believers on TV or in the newspaper, but often those portrayals are in a negative light. You may be the only one they can interact with in person. It's been said in a poem that "you are a living Bible, known and read by men." The rhyme goes on to ask, "What does the Bible say, 'according to you'?"

So are you exhibiting a proper representation of Christianity? Are you kind, thoughtful, and approachable? What would people say about God based on what they see of your life? What does the Bible say, according to you?

*Father, this sounds like such a responsibility! Are You sure You want me to be Your representative? But I'm willing, Lord—please speak to others through my words and actions. Amen.*

# Well Done!

There is coming a day when your time on earth will end. But hopefully that won't be true about your influence as a man after God's own heart. No, as you are faithful to pour your life into your family, your friends, your workmates, and fellow believers at church, your influence will live on in their lives. You'll be gone, but God's work done through you will continue. You, as His messenger, will no longer speak, but God's message will live on.

May you never lose sight of the calling to live as a man after God's own heart. For in the end, you'll get the greatest reward anyone could ever hope to receive—that of hearing the Lord Jesus Christ say to you, "Well done, good and faithful servant."

*God, I don't know how many decades I will have to serve You, but I do know I have today. When this very day ends, may I sense You whispering, "Well done." Amen.*

# Other Books by Jim George

### The Bare Bones Bible® Handbook

The perfect resource for a fast and friendly overview of every book of the Bible. Includes the grand theme and main points of each book, the key men and women of God and what you can learn from them, the major events in Bible history, and personal applications for spiritual growth and daily living.

### The Bare Bones Bible® Handbook for Teens

Based on the bestselling *Bare Bones Bible® Handbook*, this edition includes content and life applications specially written with teens in mind! They will be amazed at how much the Bible has to say about the things that matter most to them—their happiness, friends and family, home and school, and goals for the future. Great for youth group studies!

### Know Your Bible from A to Z

Bible teacher Jim George leads you through a concise and easy-to-understand A-to-Z survey of the Bible's most important people, places, customs, and events. Along the way, you'll discover how to apply the Scriptures to your daily life, helping you know what God wants for you.

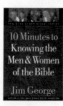

### 10 Minutes to Knowing the Men and Women of the Bible

The lessons you can learn from the outstanding men and women of the Bible are powerfully relevant for today. As you review their lives through the biographical sketches in this book, you'll discover special qualities worth emulating and life lessons for everyday living, which will energize your spiritual growth.

### A Leader After God's Own Heart

What makes a man a truly good leader—one God can use? Jim George looks at 15 ways to lead with strength, and to have a positive and lasting impact on others.

### A Man After God's Own Heart

Many Christian men want to be men after God's own heart…but how do they do this? George shows that a heartfelt desire to practice God's priorities is all that's needed. God's grace does the rest. Includes study guide. This book has appeared on the Evangelical Christian Booksellers Association's bestseller list.

### A Husband After God's Own Heart

Husbands will find their marriages growing richer and deeper as they pursue God and discover 12 areas in which they can make a real difference in their relationship with their wife. (This book was a 2005 Gold Medallion Award Finalist.)

### The Man Who Makes a Difference

What made the apostle Paul so effective, so influential? Readers will experience true fulfillment as they learn how they can make a real and lasting difference in the workplace, at home, at church, and in their community.

### A Young Man After God's Own Heart

Pursuing God really *is* an adventure—a lot like climbing a mountain. There are all kinds of challenges on the way up, but the awesome view at the top is well worth the trip. This book helps teen men to experience the thrill of knowing real success in life—the kind that counts with God. (This book was a 2006 Gold Medallion Award Finalist.)

### A Young Man's Guide to Making Right Choices

This book will help teen men to think carefully about their decisions, assuring a more fulfilling and successful life. A great resource for gaining the skills needed to face life's challenges.

### A Young Man's Guide to Discovering His Bible

God's Word can change a young man's life—for real. But that can't happen until he commits himself to knowing the Bible. This book will help teen guys to discover what Scripture says and make it their personal guide.

### A Boy After God's Own Heart

This book helps boys learn how to make good decisions and great friends, see the benefits of homework and chores, get along better with their parents and siblings, and get into the Bible and grow closer to God.

### A Boy's Guide to Making Really Good Choices

What a difference good choices can make! Helping a boy to understand how to make good choices will take him some very big steps toward growing up. This book helps boys to make good decisions about what they say, how they spend their time, who they choose as friends, what they watch and read, and more.

### A Boy's Guide to Discovering His Bible

Through the Bible's many adventures and teachings, God speaks about how He desires for His children to live. In this book boys will learn both helpful and fun ways to better understand their Bible.

### A Little Boy After God's Own Heart
(*coauthored with Elizabeth George*)
With delightful artwork by Judy Luenebrink, this book encourages young boys in the virtues of patience, goodness, faithfulness, sharing, and more. Written to help boys discover how special they are, these rhymes present wisdom and character traits for life.

### God's Wisdom for Little Boys
(*coauthored with Elizabeth George*)
The wonderful teachings of Proverbs come to life for boys. Memorable rhymes play alongside colorful paintings for an exciting presentation of truths to live by.

## About the Author

Jim George is a teacher and speaker and an award-winning, bestselling author of numerous books, including *A Man After God's Own Heart* and *The Bare Bones Bible® Handbook*. To order any of his books, visit:

www.JimGeorge.com